MONKEES ARCHIVES 3

MONKEES
ARCHIVES VOL 3

White Lightning Publishing
Copyright ©2016 White Lightning Publishing

This volume reprints artifacts related to the Monkees. Through research, we believe that all pieces to be in the public domain. If you hold valid and current copyrights presented, please contact us at WhiteLightningPublishing@gmail.com with proof so that we can remove materials on future printings.

MONKEES ARCHIVES 3

Geo A. Hamid PROUDLY PRESENTS
STEEL PIER
MAGAZINE

THE AMUSEMENT CITY AT SEA

SCENE OF THE FABULOUS GOLDEN DOME

THE SHOW PLACE OF THE NATION

DAILY TIME SCHEDULE OF EVENTS

ATLANTIC CITY, NEW JERSEY

25¢

MONKEES ARCHIVES 3

MONKEES ARCHIVES 3

MONKEES ARCHIVES 3

MONKEES ARCHIVES 3

MONKEES ARCHIVES 3

MONKEES ARCHIVES 3

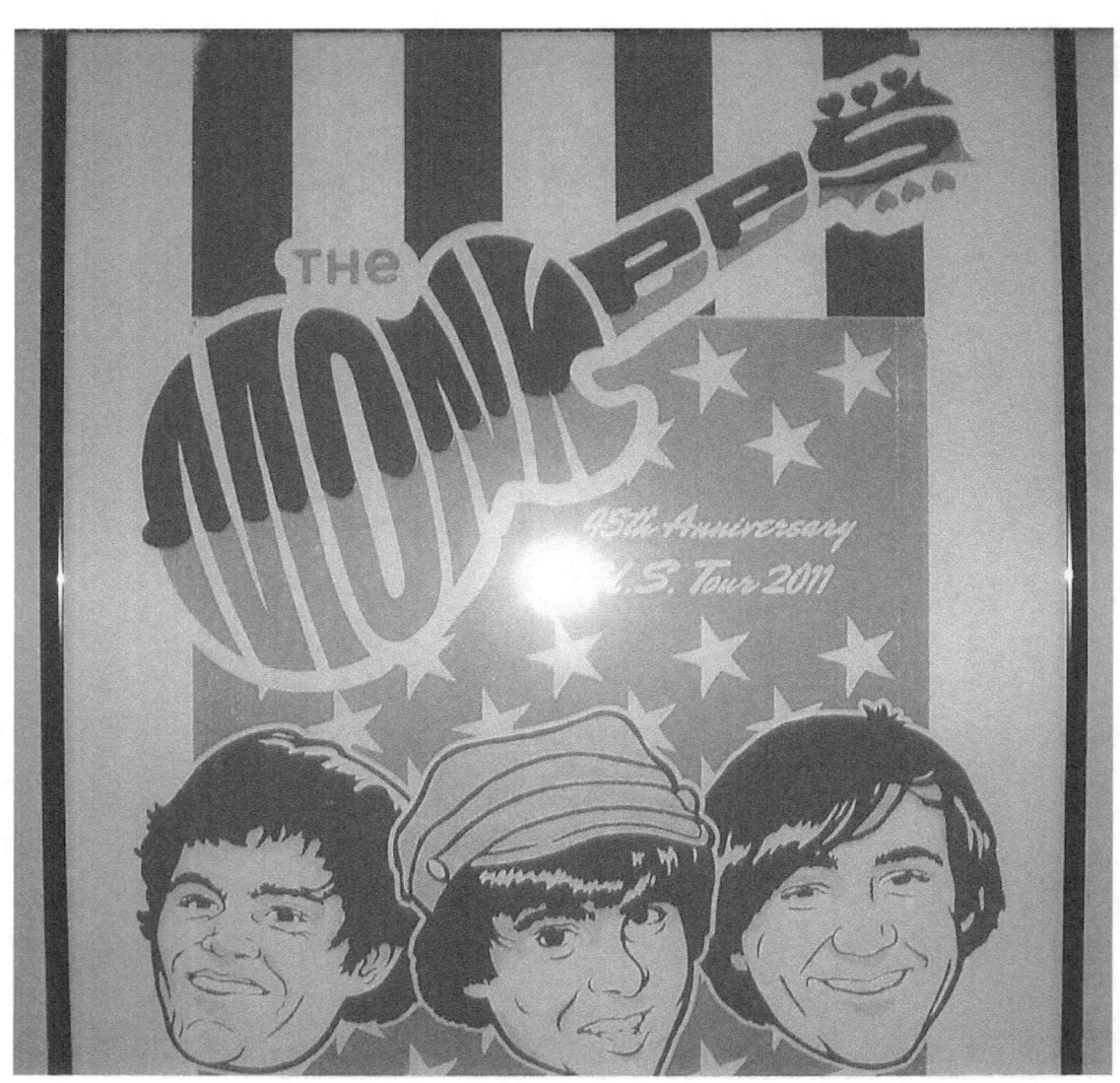

MONKEES ARCHIVES 3

MONKEES ARCHIVES 3

MONKEES ARCHIVES 3

MONKEES ARCHIVES 3

MONKEES ARCHIVES 3

MONKEES ARCHIVES 3

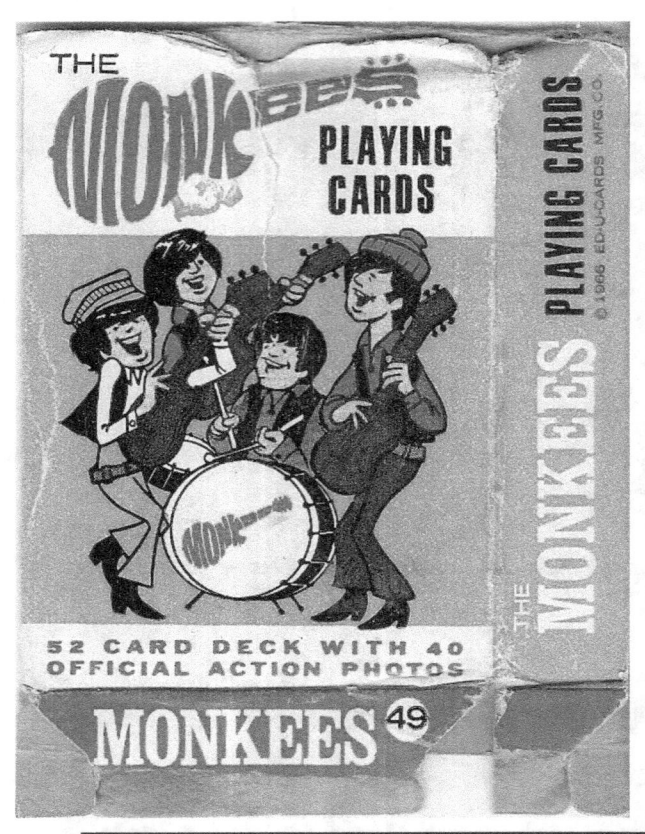
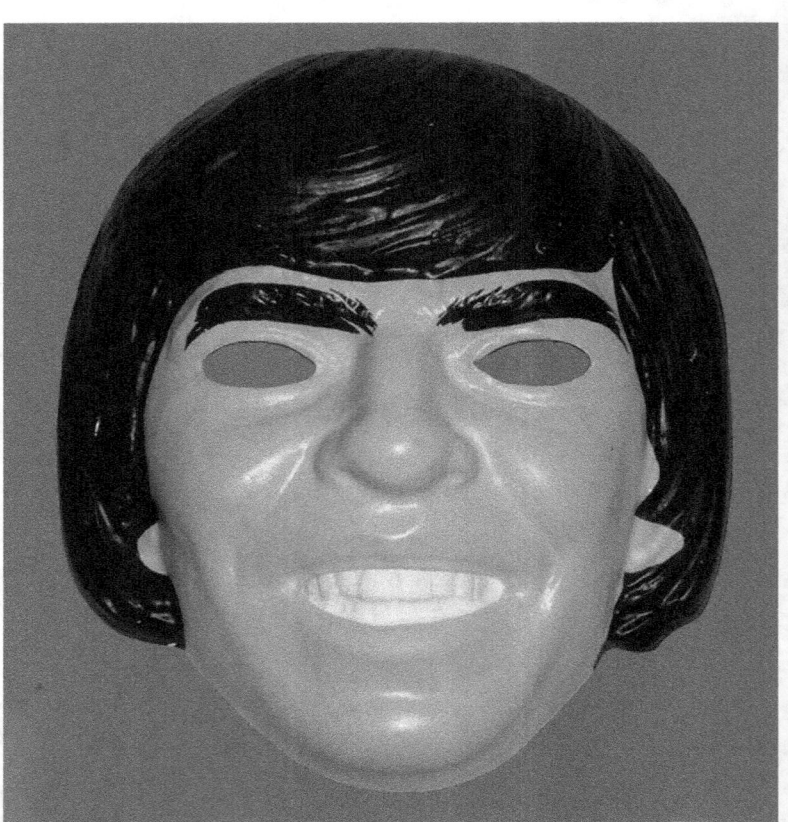

MONKEES ARCHIVES 3

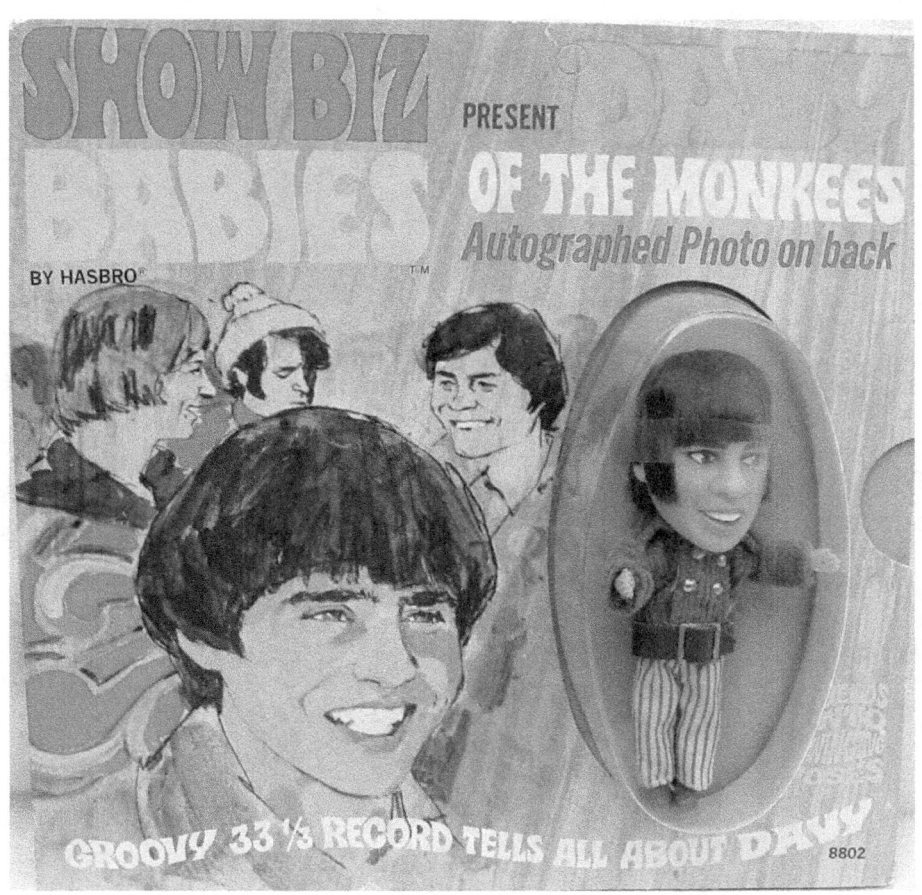

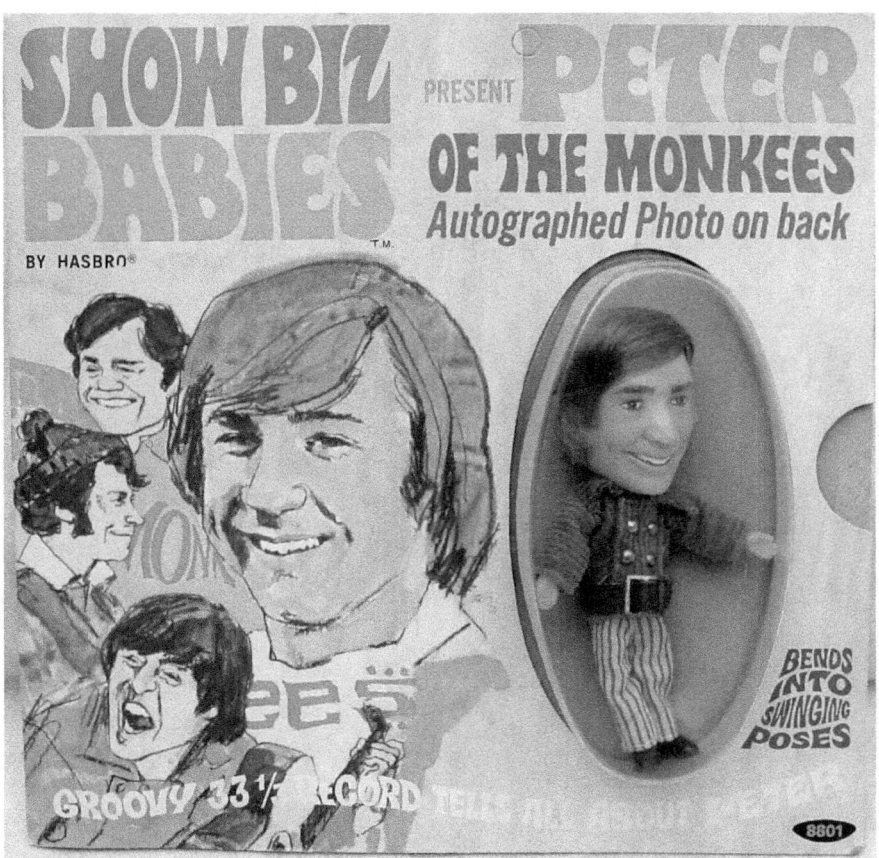

MONKEES ARCHIVES 3

MONKEES ARCHIVES 3

MONKEES ARCHIVES 3

THE MONKEEMOBILE ©

Hey, Hey, we're the Monkees! And the Monkees liked to travel together, kind of like the four Monkeeteers, to coin a phrase. And, not wanting to drive in some ordinary "wimpmobile" or just your everyday muscle car, they opted for a full tilt radical custom of the Car of Cars, a 1967 GTO. This stylish wonder features a full Phaeton style stretched out interior with a stem-to-stern canvas top for full cover shade, a radical GTO monster motor mill complete with a custom "huffer" and four exhaust trumpets per side, neatly exiting out behind the custom front wheels-n-tires playing out in quad stereo the tune this monster motor makes. And speaking of tunes, the Monkee name is emblazened along both sides of the car so you have no doubt who it is in the radical red beast. Hey, Hey, we're the Monkees!

© 1989 Columbia Pictures Industries, Inc.

Stock No. 6058
Form No. 099-6058
Printed in the United States

HEY! HEY! HERE COMES THE MODEL CAR SCIENCE MAD MOD MONKEEMOBILE CONTEST

WITH ENOUGH LOOT FOR 50 WINNERS!

FIRST PRIZE .... **$100 SAVINGS BOND**
SECOND THRU TENTH PRIZE .. **ALBUM OF THE GREATEST MONKEE MUSIC**
ELEVENTH THRU FIFTIETH PRIZE .. **MPC'S FORD J-CAR KIT**

ALL YOU HAVE TO DO IS BUILD A MONKEE MACHINE ANYWAY YOU WANT IT... STOCK, SCRATCH-BUILT, OR CUSTOM. THEN PAINT IT UP AS WILD AS YOUR MOD MIND CAN HANDLE. GO OP, POP, FOG, FLAME, OR MAYBE EVEN PAISLEY! JUST MAKE IT SO "IN" THAT IT'S INDUBITABLY "OUT-A-SIGHT". RUSH US A COLOR PHOTO OF YOUR VERSION OF THE BOSS BUGGY, AND YOU'RE IN ON THE ACTION!

CONTEST CLOSES MAY 31ST, 1967. ALL PHOTOS BECOME THE PROPERTY OF MODEL CAR SCIENCE. SEND YOUR ENTRIES TO: "THE MCS MONKEE CONTEST," 131 BARRINGTON PLACE, WEST LOS ANGELES, CALIFORNIA 90049.

MONKEES ARCHIVES 3

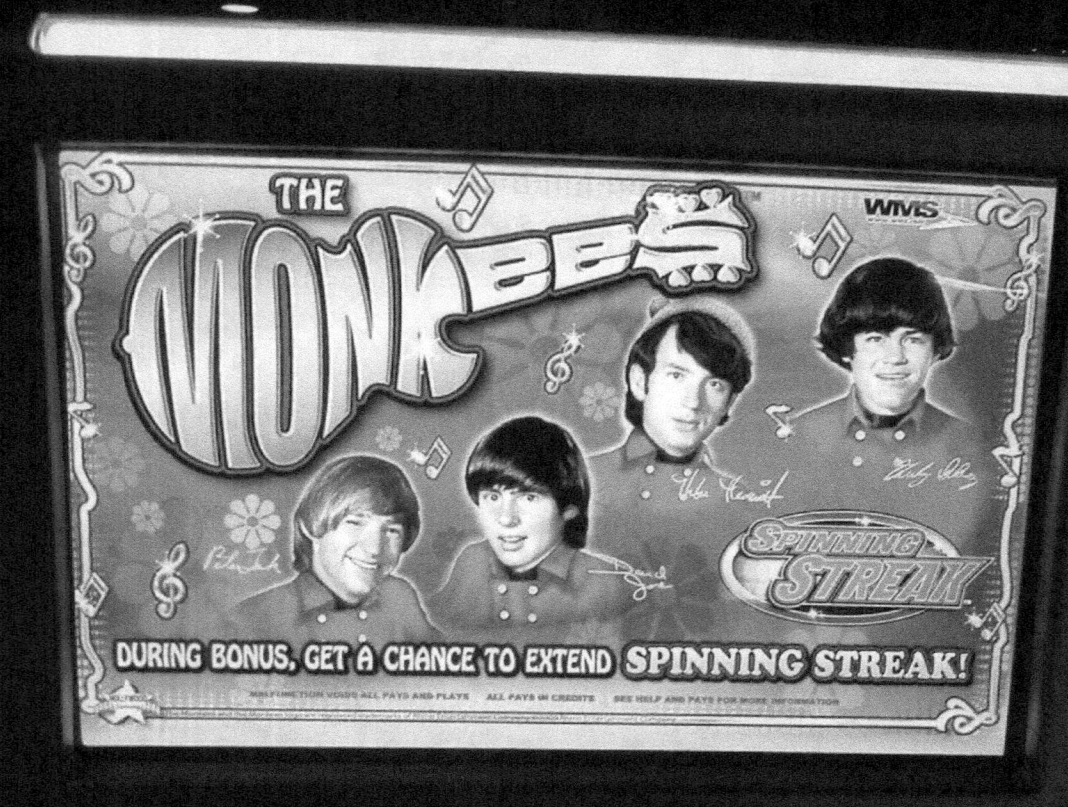

MONKEES ARCHIVES 3

MONKEES ARCHIVES 3

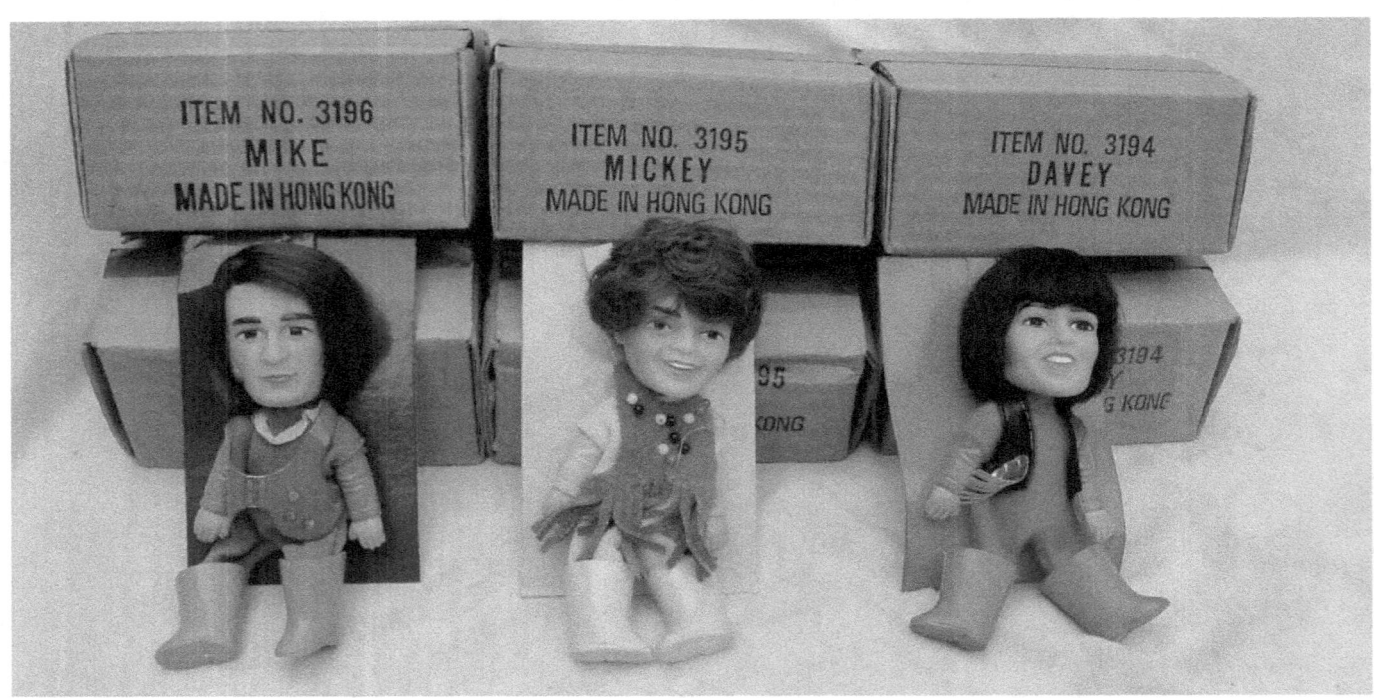

MONKEES ARCHIVES 3

Tonight's special traces The Monkees from their "creation" by a way-out sorcerer to their current eminence. The Monkees will be joined by guests Julie Driscoll; Brian Auger and the Trinity; Jerry Lee Lewis; Fats Domino; Little Richard; the Clara Ward Singers; the Buddy Miles Express; Paul Arnold and the Moon Express; and the We Three Trio.

8 PM IN COLOR NBC 4

MONKEES ARCHIVES 3

tv CHANNELS

DAILY LISTINGS ■ AUG. 6-AUG. 12, 1967

Detroit Free Press
WEEKLY tv MAGAZINE

A visit with Emmy-Winning Frances Bavier

SMOOTH SAILING FOR THE MONKEES

MONKEES ARCHIVES 3

MONKEES ARCHIVES 3

Making music: Davy Jones, Micky Dolenz, Peter Tork and Mike Nesmith.

THE GREAT REVOLT OF '67

Wherein The Monkees, finally a group, battled and won the right to play their own music

BY DWIGHT WHITNEY

At Screen Gems they call it No Man's Land. It is given a wide berth by the Studio's Sta-Prest pants set. It is a shabby green building, converted from a duplex apartment—its walls scuffed, its steps in a crumbling state of disrepair—crammed between buildings at the far end of the parking lot. On the wall of the cluttered second-floor reception room is a sign which says *War Is Not Healthy for Children and Other Living Beings*, an ancient advertisement for a Lydia Pinkham Calumet Corset Clasp, and a photograph of LBJ bearing the legend, *He Who Meddles in a Quarrel is like One Who Takes a Passing Dog by the Ears. Proverbs 26:17*.

This is GHQ for The Monkees. The Monkees are the creation, in the image of The Beatles, of two ambitious young men named Bert Schneider, 34, and Robert Rafelson, 33, the former the son of the president of Columbia Pictures, of which Screen Gems is the TV arm. Schneider and Rafelson advertised in the Hollywood trade papers for "four insane boys, 17-21, with the courage to work," found them, and through the marvelous alchemy of TV converted them into the hottest new act in show business—an accomplishment rendered all the more remarkable by the fact that the boys could not play their instruments well enough to record the hit tunes that made them famous. Someone else did it for them. Act? Well, they didn't really act either: They "romped," to use their director's favorite term.

It wasn't easy, of course. True creation never is. First off you have to have the whole hippie movement going for you. You must acknowledge that the world is divided into two parts: (1) the turned-on people, the flower children—the seekers and true believers who dig the mind-blown scene; and (2) the up-tight straight world of people over 30 with their square Hawaiian sports shirts, their down-trip attitudes and their Sta-Prest ideas of what the world is all about. You have to have been a student of a movie called "A Hard Day's Night," starring The Beatles, which established the ground rules for making this wacky, way-out musical scene back in 1964. Since your four insane boys are generally bereft of anything resembling professionalism, you have to invent a whole "subjective" routine for them, a kind of Freudian free-association thing in which they tell you what it feels like to be a teapot while riding a motorcycle standing up; and you photograph it all with a hand-held camera. You have to figure out a "sound" for them, too, since they either can't, or you don't trust them to, figure it out for themselves. You import professionals, placing in charge of the whole musical operation a young Galahad of the record wars named Donny Kirshner, described as "the Dr. Timothy Leary of sound," strictly a man with a telephone in his Cadillac.

Now you are holding all the aces —you hope—in a four-way game involving huge profits in records, a TV show (which is really a kind of super-promo for the record sales), personal appearances and merchandising. You have galvanized the entire resources of a TV-and-movie-making studio behind you. The studio is making, Kirshner is making, you are making (or stand to make) millions. Your boys— "corporate pawns," one of your record producers once had the poor taste to call them—are making a quick $500 a week. But that doesn't really matter when you consider their collective 5 percent of the record take, not to mention their cut of the merchandising (10 percent of Raybert Productions' share) or the fat pickings (30 percent of the net) they stand to make from the Hawaiian, European and American tours (on their first try they netted $40,000 each from nine play dates)—if they can teach themselves to play their instruments well enough to handle it all.

There is just one thing wrong with the picture. The dream is built on a house of cards. The TV Establishment is not ready for The Monkees: worse yet, The Monkees are not ready

—→

for the Establishment. Young, frightened, confused, they are entirely unschooled in the nuances of handling a big success. They are thumped, bumped and rattled around like marbles in a tin tub, fearful that someone will discover them for what they are: four not very secure boys named Davy Jones, ex-Newmarket jockey turned stage singer; Micky Dolenz, ex-child star of *Circus Boy*; Peter Tork (nee Thorkelson), an economics professor's son, who once played the coffee-house circuit; and Mike Nesmith, onetime protest singer—all of whom sense with increasing discomfort that they are being manipulated.

Suddenly there are too many people pulling on them, expecting things that they do not know how to deliver. They are expected to "break up the whole damn scene—that's the way to get publicity!" In their nervousness they begin to compete with each other to see who can say the "funniest" things. *Understand you have a wife, Mr. Nesmith? . . . Uh, yeah, she's got a hairy chest and is a good basketball player . . .* Once they entertain a lady teen-scene journalist by playing catch with the salad.

Then disaster strikes. The scene is Chasen's restaurant in late June 1966, before the first *Monkees* show reaches the public. NBC is entertaining its affiliates, the men who decide what their stations will carry, and stars of the new fall shows are making appearances. While the whole hippie movement has by this time gained wide acceptance in American life, the affiliates are conservative, skeptical men, known to be opposed on principle to anything long-haired.

"Bert Schneider was against the boys' going," recalls a behind-the-scenes participant. "He figured it for a square scene and the affiliates wouldn't dig it anyway. But the network insisted; the affiliates had to be won over. The head writers had a sketch for them, and the boys were supposed to kind of come in on the end of things, make a quick appearance and get out.

"But things ran late. They stood outside, tired, nervous, unfed. I said, 'Are you guys going to do the material?' 'Hell, no,' they said. Somebody had dragged along a stuffed peacock. They played volleyball with it, stopping traffic on Beverly Boulevard. Micky got into the restaurant's switch box and turned off all the lights. Finally they were introduced by Dick Clark. Since they hadn't any musical instruments—we were afraid to let 'em try to play—they did 'comedy' material. Micky shaved with the microphone. Davy pretended he was a duck. The jokes began to die. The affiliates were already hostile and what was not needed was a bunch of smart-aleck kids.

"On the way out I heard an affiliate say, 'That's *The Monkees*? Forget it.'"

The network was later to pay dearly for this unseemly display. At least five key stations failed to pick up the show, resulting in national ratings which did not accurately reflect its true popularity. In the studio it caused a widening of the rift between pro- and anti-Monkee factions.

The Chasen's fiasco did another thing, too. It suddenly attracted the attention of the big-time press. Schneider, who believed he could "control" the press, held the news hounds at bay as long as he could. But by midsummer he was in the soup. He had four boys but no music. Kirshner, the president of Colgems—a new subsidiary of Screen Gems' music division especially created for the Monkee music and in which, significantly, RCA Victor had an interest—arrived in town and quickly decided that he must use professional musicians to "create" The Monkees sound. He came up with "Last Train to Clarksville," by Tommy

MONKEES ARCHIVES 3

Boyce and Bobby Hart.

"I heard them. They were loud," Kirshner recalls, of his first exposure to The Monkees. "It was not the right sound. Not a young, happy, driving, pulsating sound of today. I wanted a musical sex image. Something you'd recognize next time you heard it. Davy was OK—for musical comedy. Mike was the weakest singer as far as I was concerned. Micky was a natural mimic. And he had the best voice for our purposes. He did the lead on 'Last Train.' Davy and Peter sang some background harmony. Mike wasn't on the record at all. Boyce and Hart and hand-picked professional musicians played it. The boys told me, 'Donny, anything you want to do is OK with us.'

"Later we tried Mike on the lead of 'I'm a Believer.' We had to take him off." It was the beginning of their disenchantment.

By September, Kirshner's "Last Train" was on its way to the top of the record charts, where it would remain for an embarrassingly long time. But, thanks in part to the Chasen's affair, Schneider's newly minted TV show was residing in the bottom half of the Nielsen charts.

Indeed the situation was trying for Schneider. His autocratic attitude ("People over 30 are square!") infuriated the rest of the studio. Reporters were treated like Russian spies. Consequently he had the press on his neck; the New York Times was about to leak the first story hinting at the boys' musical ineptitude. And he was facing the constant threat that his boys, increasingly aware of their power, might explode at any time.

Kirshner, by his apparent unwillingness to treat them as anything but overgrown children, was not helping this along any. To make matters worse, Kirshner had 15 percent of Colgems' net profits before taxes. Since some 6,000,000 singles and 8,000,000 albums had been sold by midseason, Donny was growing rich. The boys had to struggle along on a 1.25 percent royalty apiece, a fair piece of change, but minuscule next to the $300,000 Kirshner had already made and the upwards of $5,000,000 he stood to make from the Monkees operation over a five-year period.

The Monkees were, moreover, artistically hung up: "The music on our records has nothing to do with us," the spokesman for the group, intense young Mike Nesmith, had said once and was ready to say again. "It's totally dishonest. We don't record our own music. Tell the world we're synthetic because, dammit, we are! We want to play our own."

It was not so much an ultimatum as an agonized cry. Because what they really craved was that good old-fashioned "straight" attribute—acceptance. They just didn't know how to go about getting it. Their pride was hurt. They were increasingly aware that it was The Beatles, The Byrds, The Mamas and the Papas to whom the musical world looked with genuine if sometimes grudging admiration. At the Monterey International Pop Festival it was those darlings of the Haight-Ashbury crowd, The Jefferson Airplane and The Grateful Dead, who mind-blew the hip crowd. The Monkees felt like clowns.

In the beginning they accepted this limitation dutifully. Before the show started shooting in June 1966, they were being trained as "improvisational" actors and taking a crash course in the musical fundamentals. What made the music situation doubly impossible was that they were acting 10 to 12 hours a day. Since no music recording is ever done on a set—the actors "lip-sync" the words to a playback—there simply was not time for amateur experimentation.

Thus the boys were frustrated by the very system that enriched them.

→

Still, they had to become proficient enough to get by on the concert stage, where no musical stand-ins were possible.

They practiced feverishly, put a saddle on their jumping nerves and, with the help of a planeload of equipment and some psychedelic stage effects whomped up for them by choreographer David Winters, opened in Honolulu on Dec. 3. "They were a smash," reports one eyewitness. "The music? With all those screaming kids, who can tell?"

Meantime, the love-match between the boys and Kirshner ("To the man who made it all possible," read the inscription on the 48x48 photograph they had given him in the fall) was starting to decline. It began with Mike Nesmith. Mike fancied himself not only a musician, but a record producer and composer as well. Kirshner, a rough-and-tumble musical pragmatist to the lapels of his Sy Devore suit, rode a narrow line between tolerating and patronizing them. He listened—but not very hard—to the tapes they recorded on their own in the naive hope that one of them would please "Donny." He made vague promises that (the boys later claimed) he never kept. The father-figure image, once exclusively Kirshner's province, was shifting back onto producer Schneider, a self-styled overage (34) up-tripper who was more adept at telling the boys what they wanted to hear.

Clearly a showdown was coming. And come it did. Surprisingly, it also produced an emotion-packed confrontation between Kirshner and the boys, who were tired of being "corporate pawns," stung by the taunts of their musician friends and scorned in the press as being the rock 'n' roll group that didn't rock and didn't roll.

In late January 1967 The Monkees met with Kirshner in his $150-a-day bungalow suite in that swank bastion of Hollywood squaredom, the Beverly Hills Hotel. They had come to plead their case with their once-adored mentor. Kirshner was on the spot. RCA Victor, which distributes Colgems records, was pressuring him for a third single and album. He needed the boys and yet—well, uh, he didn't need them. He was flanked by his henchmen from the studio music division, Lester Sill and Herb Moelis; and, to make it even more grotesque, had four Gold Records, those coveted totems of million-copy record sales, ready to present to the boys. The Monkees were alone; Schneider wisely had stayed home.

Gingerly they came on with their demands: that they play their own instruments, choose their own songs; Kirshner would oversee. Mike later described Kirshner's reaction as "a little uneasiness, the sweaty-palms-in-the-eye syndrome." Kirshner replied that he had prepared four demos (test records) of possible tunes for them to record; he added a short, blunt recapitulation of the facts of life of the music business. Mike flushed and turned on Kirshner.

"Donny," he said, "we could sing 'Happy Birthday' with a beat and it would sell a million records. [Your argument] is no longer valid because we are The Monkees and we have that incredible TV exposure."

When Kirshner, unnerved, backed off, Mike threatened to quit. Herb Moelis said, "You'd better read your contract." Mike whitened with rage. He disliked Moelis ("Why? Why do I dislike strawberry ice cream? He didn't respect me as an artist!"). Then he smashed his fist through the wall of Kirshner's $150-a-day bungalow. Kirshner caught up with Mike in the lobby and thrust the Gold Record upon him. Lester Sill drove Mike, clutching the Gold Record and smoldering, home.

Later Mike told his "angel of peace," the ever-conciliatory Schneider, "I

MONKEES ARCHIVES 3

blew it. I shouldn't've lost my temper. But it's horrible to be No. 1 group in the country and not be allowed to play your own records." Schneider said, "Well, it's rewarding to see you guys act as a group rather than four egotists who don't pull together."

To which Mike replied, "It's the first time we've had one wagon to pull."

From then on the situation deteriorated rapidly, with the other boys falling in line behind Mike. "Bert knew I meant it when I said I'd quit the whole complex, pack up my gear, go to Mexico or Tahiti, eat coconuts and let everybody sue me." Amazingly, Schneider believed him, the studio believed him. The ever-realistic Kirshner obviously didn't. It was just too incredible. But less than a month later Kirshner was out, flower-power was in, and Screen Gems and Columbia Pictures had law-suits totalling $35,500,000 on their hands—what Donny Kirshner figured the rude abrogation of his contract was worth.

The boys took off on a much-needed vacation, returning a few weeks later to, of all places, a sound-recording stage. The new album, "Headquarters," is, for better or worse, all theirs. Mike said, "It makes the group tighter and closer and proud as punch . . ." And zap! Happy Birthday! There it was, right at the top of the charts, just one notch below The Beatles! The up-tight world of straights with their Sta-Prest pants defeated at last! It was a good, heady, up-trip feeling. And Nesmith was pleased to recall that transcendental moment when, listening to the car radio later in the spring, he first heard the real, genuine bona-fide Monkees doing their thing on "The Girl I Knew Somewhere." Groovy! Super-zappy! Mind-blowing! Cosmic! Mike honked the horn impatiently for his wife and his friend and his brother-in-law to come out. "Hey," he yelled, "want to sit in on a moment in *history*?"

MONKEES ARCHIVES 3

MIKE & DAVY "GO TO

Mike with his two very precious dogs: Frak, an attack-trained Shepherd, and Spotte, a retriever.

Frak, despite his training, is a very loving dog and Mike and Phyllis are especially fond of him.

Friends of the Nesmiths, like Bill Martin, are known by Frak and Spotte—and treated like friends!

As Frak goes back under the house, Spotte stays at Mike's side.

"THE DOGS!"

Meanwhile, across town, Davy is relaxing with his Shepherd, Suzy!

Suzy, like *his* master (for an explanation of *that*, see last month's FLIP!), is friendly, playful and lots of frisky fun!

Suzy lets Davy know how he feels about the Jones boy!

Now you can order

DAVY'S FIRST LP
Stores can't get it!

DAVY SINGS EVERY SONG
A RARE COLLECTOR'S ALBUM
HURRY! SUPPLY LIMITED
(Please order only as many as you need!)

☐ Send me_____ NEW DAVY LP(s)
Enclose $5.75 for each.

Send this ad with your name
& address with Zip Code & money to:
DAVY'S FIRST LP
P.O. BOX 3031 F
HOLLYWOOD, CALIF. 90028

SEND 50c FOR RUSH HANDLING

MONKEES ARCHIVES 3

Micky invites you to come along with him as he has a roof-rave! Micky took time out for this foto fling while The Monkees were in Portland.

YOU TRAVEL WITH ME AND THE MONKEES! BY RIC KLEIN

TUESDAY/DALLAS

We flew here from Des Moines, and headquartered at the Cabana Hotel. Mike's friends were all on hand, of course, when we arrived because this is his part of the world. Mike spent a lot of time with them, while most of us just goofed around the pool. We decided to build a HUMAN PYRAMID in the pool! David Pearl, Micky and Mike Graber (Mike's hairdresser) were on the

MONKEES ARCHIVES 3

bottom, a couple of The Sundowners and I were in the middle, and Davy clambered to the peak of the pyramid! It worked for a couple of seconds until we all splashed into the pool!

A photographer should never face the sun—except when another photographer wants to take his pic! Which is why Micky happily turned around for best friend Ric Klein's FLIP lens!

WEDNESDAY/DALLAS

The day of the concert at Memorial Auditorium. Seemed as if Mike was bringing half of Texas with him! Mike took all his friends and most of his wife Phyllis' family to the concert. And they, like everyone, flipped out! It was a groovy concert.

A Monkee's never alone! Even while Micky was scampering around the hotel roof, passers-by looked on.

MONKEES ARCHIVES 3

THURSDAY/HOUSTON
This was the city where the police kept giving us a hard time. They kept throwing us out of the Sam Houston College auditorium, even though we had passes and even though the show couldn't possibly go on without the crew! David Pearl probably had the toughest time, but all of us were challenged by the police every time we made a move.

"Hi, there!"

FRIDAY/SHREVEPORT
I have two memories of Shreveport: (1) We destroyed glasses at poolside with our usual wild fun and games and (2) the crew bought Davy a soccer ball. So, he promptly went out on the field, and his team (which also had Micky on it) beat a team led by Jim Edmundson (our chief security officer). We also played a lot of football on the lawn of the Shreveporter, our motel, before our concert that night at Hirsch Memorial Collage.

SATURDAY & SUNDAY/MOBILE & DETROIT
After our concert in Mobile, we whipped off to Detroit for our concert which had been postponed because of the trouble in that city. In Detroit, it was an afternoon concert, our only one of the entire tour.

MONDAY/NASHVILLE
We didn't believe it! But our hotel was right next door to the YWCA!

Your trip with The Monkees has much more to go! Flip to Page 46!

MONKEES ARCHIVES 3

YOU TRAVEL WITH ME AND THE MONKEES!
BY RIC KLEIN

So, of course, there were girls day and night in front of the hotel. But the "Y" had declared our hotel off-limits, threatening to expel any girls who entered. Everything worked out OK, anyway, and we were delighted with our next-door neighbors!

We stayed here three days, so that Micky, Davy, Mike and Peter could get some recording sessions in. But, other than that, the guys never

MONKEES ARCHIVES 3

stayed together, making it tough for me to track them down for you.

Davy rented a Mercury convertible and did a lot of antique shopping. Mike bought about $900 worth of rifles, and Micky and Davy each bought one, too, only to discover that there was no place to go shooting! They did go on a picnic, though, at a farm just outside of Nashville. But ants aren't any fun to shoot at!

THURSDAY/MEMPHIS
We were scheduled to arrive early in the day, but were late and didn't get to the Admiral Benbow Inn until late in the day. Davy played golf with a local DJ and Jim Edmundson, our security man. And Mike, Micky and Peter went to Stack's—Memphis' famous recording studios. Booker T & The MGs are the studio recording group there, and the guys watched them record. Peter carried his own little tape recorder with him all summer, and he taped himself playing the bongos! We all had a good time in Memphis.

FRIDAY/TULSA
We were late here, too, and didn't spend much time either before or after the concert in Tulsa. But Micky did manage to pick up some leathercrafts and tools in this part of the world where the Indian influence is great. All the boys, by the way, made beads throughout the tour. They have bead looms and, whenever they have a minute or are in the mood, they'll work on them.

SATURDAY/DENVER
Our concert here was the last one before we took five days off in Los Angeles. And it was something

Mike looked out of the hotel window in Portland to discover he was looking right into FLIP's candid camera! So, what did the most serious Monkee of all do? Gag it up spectacularly! Would you believe Mike Nesmith...smiling?

MONKEES ARCHIVES 3

else! First, David Pearl came on stage with Mike's hat carefully tucked on top of a white pillow, like a King's crown or something! Then Neko came out with four cotton candy sticks! Mike stuck his in the end of his guitar, as my pics show, and all the guys ate them between songs. Also, each Monkee had a foot-long flower. Mike had his in his guitar, Mick carried his, Peter wore his flower and Davy also carried his flower. Towards the end of the show, we threw the flowers out into the audience. Every Monkee show on the tour was outasite, but this one in Denver was just a little more special than most!

SUNDAY-THURSDAY/LOS ANGELES

This was the week that was! The first complete week off during the whole summer! And we all took personal advantage of it. Micky had had his whole family in Denver,

Davy bought some fish lines and bait, and went fishing. Right out of his hotel window! Didn't catch anything, but had lots of fun trying!

and he went off with them to spend some time with relatives in San Jose during this free week. Davy spent a lot of his time looking for a beach house near Malibu. Malibu is one of the prettiest beaches in the world, and Davy would love to find a quiet escape there. Peter also was looking for a house on the beach, but he was looking for a permanent one. He'd love to get out of the city and live at the water's edge full time. It's only about a half hour's drive from the Screen Gems Studio on Beachwood Drive in Hollywood to the ocean, so Peter could easily make it his home. But, as I'm writing this, neither Peter nor Davy had yet found what they were looking for. Mike spent the week quietly with Phyllis and Christian at home, taking it easy, shopping and generally just catching his breath.

FRIDAY/SEATTLE

After the restful week at home, we just had three more concerts to go — our 31st, 32nd and 33rd of the summer! Seattle has a beautiful waterfront and on the afternoon of the concert, the guys went down to the waterfront and bought fishing

MONKEES ARCHIVES 3

Mad as ever, Micky practically jumped into the water for our camera!

lines and bait. No one caught anything but everyone had a good time. I think we also had a dandy shaving cream fight here in Seattle, although it may have been in Portland, which was our next stop.

SATURDAY/PORTLAND

On the way to Portland we had a "little" pillow fight, just three or four pillows were tossed until we decided to call a temporary truce. In Portland, Davy almost got into a real fight. He and David Pearl and some others had managed to elude our own security people, to spend some time on their own. But they ran into three rather unfriendly guys. Davy was ready to tackle the biggest one of the lot. Happily, there was no trouble, but it was touch-and-go for a bit. Spent the rest of the day making paper planes and little paper helicopters (and maybe we had the shaving cream fight here!) before going on stage at the Memorial Coliseum that night before 12,295 happy people.

SUNDAY/SPOKANE

None of us believed it, but this was the final show of the tour! We'd all worked very hard, we were all very tired, but we were all very sorry that it was about to end. The flight from Portland had been a very, very uncomfortable one. As soon as we were in the air, our ears started popping. The pilot turned around and flew back to Portland, where it was discovered that the

Once back inside, though, Mick "shot" back at us—with his own camera!

baggage compartment was open, so the cabin hadn't been pressurized! Our second flight out of Portland made an unscheduled landing because of some mechanical problems! So, we were all kind of relieved when we finally safely made it to Spokane.

Our equipment was beginning to disintegrate, which was understandable after the beatings of thirty-three action-packed concerts! Mike, in a fantastic burst of generosity,

Ric's Monkees Diary continues on Page 58!

MONKEES ARCHIVES 3

Denver was The Monkees' final concert before a five-day holiday, and they were determined to make it an outasite happening! And it was! The funniest event of the night was when a member of the crew, Neko Chohlis, walked on stage with a tray filled with cotton candy!

Peter stuck his cotton candy into his electric organ, grabbing sweet bites in between songs!

My Monkees Diary!

By Ric Klein

donated $7000 worth of equipment to a local group.

And then it was over!

The final concert.

The flight home.

And an unbelievable summer was over!

MONKEES ARCHIVES 3

I've tried to share every moment of the tour with you. You were there whenever Davy, Mike, Peter or Micky did anything. You were backstage, on stage, off stage. You were really the fifth Monkee.

Davy, Micky, Peter and Mike will probably do between 30 and 50 concerts next year, and they'll be going to the far east early in the spring.

Here's hoping that you'll be traveling with us then.

In the meantime, there's much happening with The Monkees — and you'll be sharing it all — starting next month in a brand-new column I'll be starting in FLIP.

So, let's make a date for December 7th. I'll be waiting for you, along with Micky, Peter, Mike and Davy!

Mmmmm...does that taste good! First Davy eats a finger full of candy.

Then, he uses it as a prop during a song!

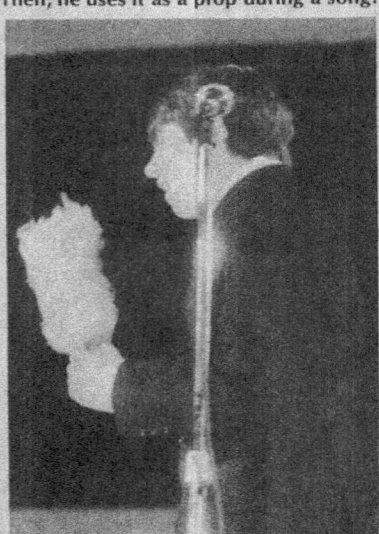

But Mike probably had the grooviest idea of all!

MONKEES ARCHIVES 3

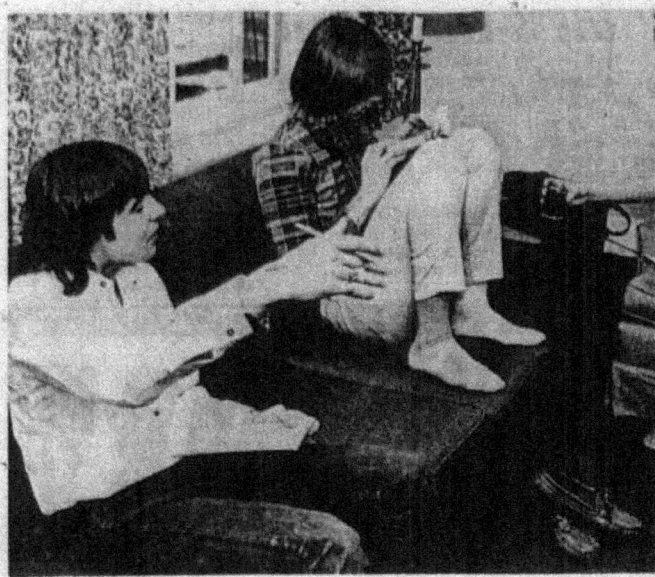
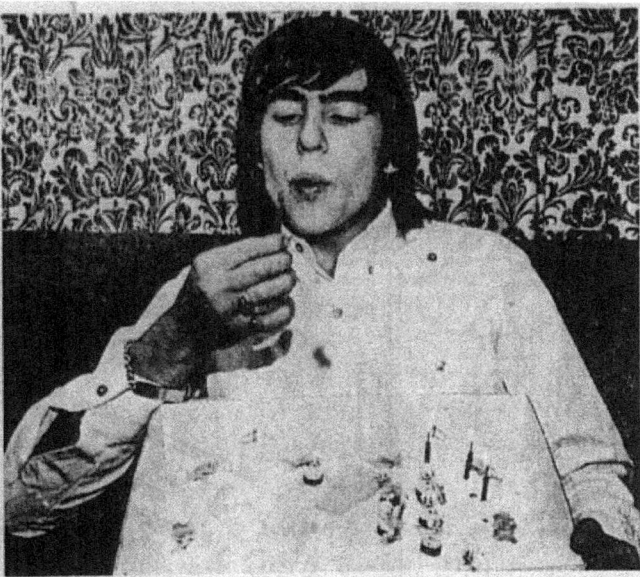

Davy Jones and barefoot Peter Tork answer questions; Davy lights up his birthday cake.

Staff Photos by Frank Jones

Monkees: Hard Workers With Varied Opinions

By Luix Overbea
Staff Reporter

It was a Monkees' world all day yesterday in the Hotel Robert E. Lee. To old folks—say over 25—there seemed to be lots of excitement and too, too many dreamy-eyed teenage girls in the lobby.

Two policemen in crisp uniforms patrolled the lobby with tolerant smiles.

From time to time, a long-hair with boots strolled through the lobby. There were squeals. "Are you with the show?" A shake of the head, and another girl was disappointed. The Monkees were not to be seen in the lobby.

With proper credentials, visitors to the hotel were permitted to ride the elevator to the ninth floor. This floor was Monkeeland.

When television's zany Monkees romped into town very early in the morning, "we were so tired," Davy Jones said, "that we did two hours of wall crawling and wall walking down the hall."

Backs to Wall

That is a kind of walking or crawling with their backs to the wall. "Anyway, we did not wake up anybody but our bosses, and who cares about that?"

Two of the four Monkees, Jones and Peter Tork, showed up for an interview. The other two, Micky Dolenz and Mike (Wool Hat) Nesmith, were at the Memorial Coliseum.

They were setting up for the show. "We have to have our amplifiers just right," Davy said in his clipped British accent. "There are some men paid to set things up, but we strive for perfection."

Jones and Tork—Davy and Peter to their television and record fans — agreed on very few things. They had opposing views on long hair and school.

On long hair:

"I look better with my hair short," Davy said. "My father doesn't like long hair. Without long hair I wouldn't have this job. So I say — people should take us for what we are, not for what's on the outside of the head, but what's in the head."

Long hair means much more to Peter. "I wore my hair long before I became a Monkee," he said. "Long hair stands for something. It says more than millions of short-hair older people have said for years."

School means a lot to Davy and something else to Peter.

"This job is important to me," Davy said. "I left school at 14. That was a big mistake. I regret it. This is the only work I know. I'm clean. I'm neat. I work because I want a job."

Flunked Out Twice

Peter, the son of two college teachers, flunked out of college twice before going into show business. He does not like school. He said:

"Look at it this way. Schools — public, private and colleges — are strictly vocational institutions. Yeah, you got to have degrees if you want to get somewhere.

"If you want to think, you do that someplace else. There is no compulsion for schools to teach knowledge. They do not teach wisdom. They do not teach people how to think."

Davy added that experience is an efficient teacher. He said, "School teaches you off the blackboard. Life teaches you firsthand through people. I have learned more through people in my six years out of school than I would have in 10 years in school."

Today Davy is 21 years old. Today is also Mike's birthday. He is 24. Somebody sent them a joint red and white birthday cake with five candles and "Happy Birthday Davy and Mike."

"Everybody sends cake," Davy said. Peter refused to pose for a picture with the cake.

Davy dresses neatly. He is so finicky that he washes his own socks and laundry.

Peter kicks off his shoes as soon as he enters a room. During the interview he wore mismatched socks, pink and yellow. "Ordinarily I don't wear pastels," he said, "but today I'm tired." He wears mismatched socks in loud colors usually.

This is the Monkees' first personal appearance tour as a group. To them it's "a gas." "It's wonderful to meet teenagers and see what they think of us," Davy said.

"Girls are fine as long as they don't get too close to us," he said. "They try to get on stage and touch you . . . talk to you. We have to be careful."

As a former stage performer in New York, Davy is more at home with the television show than the others. When the group first went on the television screen, it took them five days to film a show. Most of the shows now take 2½ to 3½ days.

They work 12 hours a day on set. "We break every rule of television," Davy said. "People are crowding on the set. Scenes are shot as we feel. This is very hard work."

All four Monkees are salaried actors. They do not get extra pay from the current personal appearance tour, taking them to 10 cities on one-night stands.

"We collect for ourselves only on records," Davy said. They have two million-seller records and one million-seller album to their credit. A new album is coming out Jan. 15.

Their personal appearances have been more taxing than they expected. In spite of the two officers in the lobby, two policemen on the ninth floor and one plainsclothesman at large, people seemed to pour in and out of the room continuously.

Everybody wanted autographs. The Monkees also gave away their album to interviewers. When reporters entered the room Davy offered them coffee or Coke.

The press conference ended with a reminder to the Monkees that they were scheduled to tour a local tobacco plant.

Goldwater's Son Hurt After Car Hits Bank

PHOENIX, Ariz. (AP) — Sheriff's officers say the car of

EDUCATOR SHOES
● GOOD SHOES ●
for all the family
KINNEY'S
● 417 N. TRADE ST—downtown
● NORTHSIDE SHOPPING CENTER

DAVY WANTS YOU TO MEET "BERT" AND "BOB"!

Normally, when Davy Jones thinks of "Bert" and "Bob" he is thinking of Bert Schneider and Bob Rafelson, The Monkees' managers and producers. These days, when Davy thinks of "Bert" and "Bob", he is thinking of his pet rabbits, whom he named after two of his favorite people. "Bert" is the grey rabbit, and "Bob" is the black one. The last we heard the real Bert and Bob were on the set of "Head," the Monkee movie, and there wasn't a carrot anywhere near them!

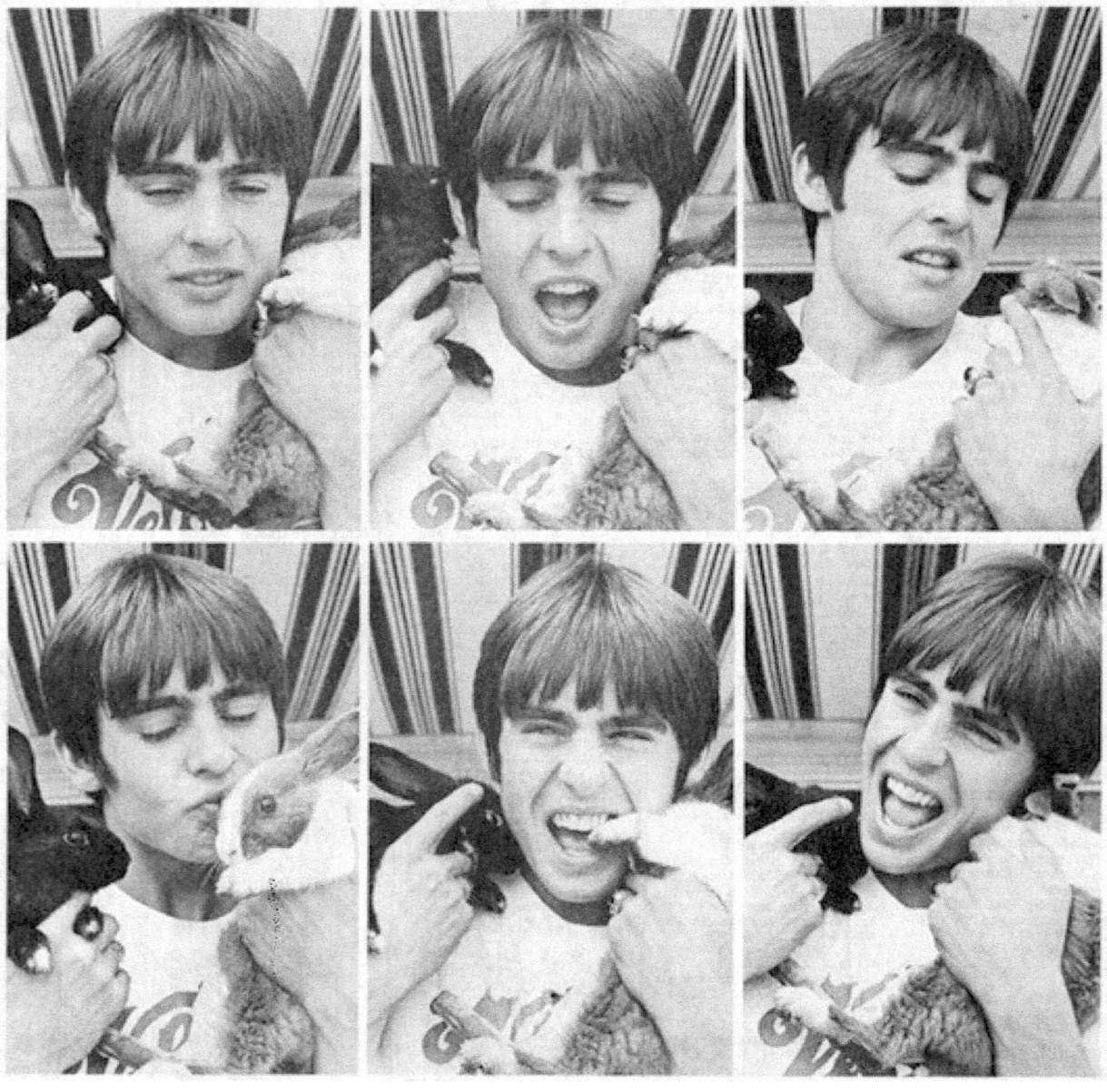

MONKEES ARCHIVES 3

Sing Along with the Monkees!

Both sides of their brand new Colgems single!!

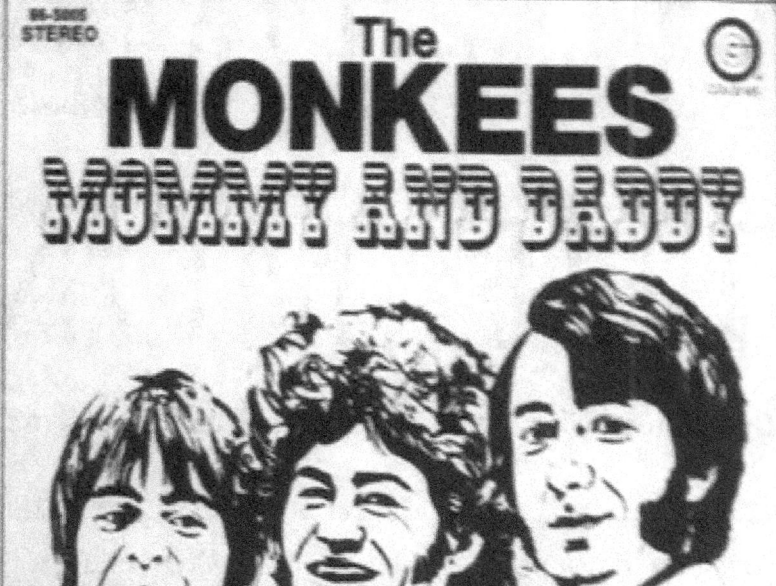

MOMMY AND DADDY

(As recorded by the Monkees on Colgems Records. Lead sung by Micky Dolenz.)

Ask your mommy and daddy
What happened to the Indian?
How come they're all living in places
With too much snow and too much sun?
Tell your mommy—
I've got a funny feeling
Deep inside of me.
Ask your daddy—
Is it really as bad
As people make it seem?

(CHORUS)
Wok taw tik-it-a tu-tu,
Wok taw tik-it-a tu-tu,
Wok taw tik-it-a tu-tu,
Wok taw tik-it-a tu-tu,
Wok taw tik-it-a.

Ask your mommy—why everybody
Swallows all those little pills?
Ask your daddy—why doesn't
That soldier care who he kills?
After they've put you to sleep
And tucked you safely down in your bed,
Whisper—"Mommy and Daddy,
would you rather that I earned it
From my friends instead?"

My questions need an answer
Or a vacuum will appear."
Dont be surprised
If they turn and walk away,
Then tell your mommy and daddy
That you love 'em anyway.

(AD LIB & FADE OUT)

(Copyright © 1969 by Screen Gems-Columbia Music, Inc. Used by Permission. Words and Music by Micky Dolenz.)

GOOD CLEAN FUN

(As recorded by the Monkees on Colgems Records. Lead sung by Michael Nesmith.)

And the sun with a kiss
Begins to dismiss
The memory of my life without you.

Well, it seems like yesterday
That my path took me away,
Although I know it's been at least a year.
But now my path heads home
And your patient time alone
Has brought me even closer to you, dear.

(CHORUS)
And this plane gets closer
Every minute I look down
To a watch that keeps lookin' back at me.
And it says to me, "Be patient, son.
You've waited this long,"
But how can I be strong?

(REPEAT CHORUS)

Well, the plane is finally down
And the engines stop their sound.
I look in the crowd and there you stand.
And the gap that once was, time
Is forever closed behind,
'Cause I told you I'd come back
And here I am.
Yes, I told you I'd come back
And here I am.

MONKEES ARCHIVES 3

FUN TIME WITH THE MONKEES

BY LYNNE RANDELL

Come along with Lynne and the guys as they storm through the South and Southwest on their American tour!

SO MUCH HAPPENS when you're with the groovy Monkees that one hardly knows where to begin—so I'll just reach out with my butterfly net and start catching dreams for you. First off, I'd like to introduce you to one of the Monkees' best friends, and probably one of the greatest hair-stylists around.

HAIRCUT LINE-UP

His name is Michael Graber (for lots more about him, see Page 14) and he went on the Monkees' summer tour to keep their "locks" in shape. Mike is one of those all-American guys we Australian girls only *hear* about. He's great-looking, tanned, and loves the sun and the surf. He's always smiling and is an excellent hairdresser. On tour, his room was more like a beauty salon than anything else. He always works in his brightly-colored surf trunks, wearing his Indian tribal beads around his neck.

You really would have fallen apart laughing if you had arrived at his door in Miami one morning, as I did. There, standing in line, were the following: Peter Tork, David Pearl and Mike Nesmith! I would say that Michael's salon was doing pretty good business, wouldn't you? Anyway, my turn finally came and he gave me a lovely trim. He has promised to dream up a groovy new hairdo for me. Hope he doesn't forget!

"FLOWER" POLICEMEN

We really had a ball in Dallas. Everywhere we went the police were very nice to us, but in Dallas they seemed especially friendly and helpful. They didn't push any of the fans around and, at the same time, they took good care of the boys. On the night of our concert there, the Monkees left the hotel carrying bouquets of mixed flowers and they gave every Dallas policeman they saw a flower to wear. It was really very nice to see those great big officers wearing white carnations and roses and the like!

While we were in Dallas, everyone on the tour took over

Peter, Mike, "Your Leader" and Davy.

Micky at work showing his color pix—while Barbara looks on.

MONKEES ARCHIVES 3

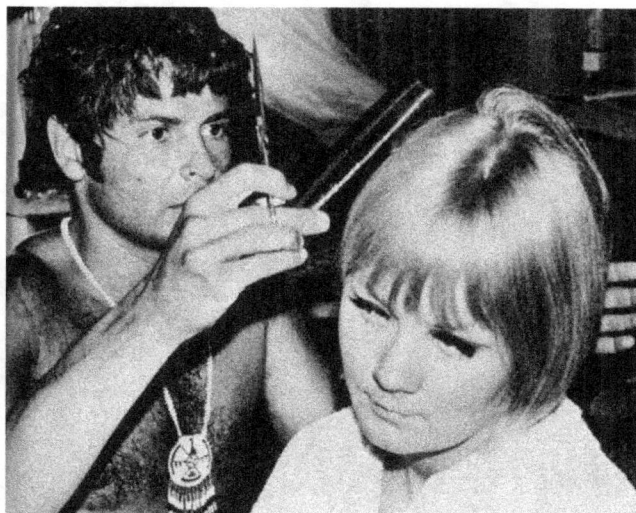

Michael "clips" Lynne.

radio station KVIL for a day. I managed to put in three hours between announcing and answering phone calls. It was rather amusing, because it was hard for me to understand that thick Texas drawl—and it was just as hard for our Texan friends to understand my funny Australian accent! The Sundowners did a turn on KVIL, and then the Monkees took over. Can you imagine what it's like to hear Micky deliver the news, Davy announce the records, Mike take over the farm reports and Peter answer the phones? Well, it came off a gas, and the deejays were so delighted that they gave us a party back at our hotel later. One KVIL deejay, who called himself "Your Leader," got on very well with the Monkees and nailed himself some fantastic interviews. If you look carefully at the picture in which he appears on this page, you'll see that Peter is wearing his famous combination——two different colored pairs of socks!

MICK DOLENZ PRESENTS—

One of the high points of our tour was a party the boys gave for Raybert V.P. Howard Sylvester's adorable secretary, Barbara Hamaker. Barbara got lovely presents from everyone on the tour—and after the party she went around "ringing merrily," wearing a necklace of bells that *16*'s editor Gloria Stavers gave her. The "program of entertainment" at Barbara's party proved to be quite unusual. Micky Dolenz showed us all the color pictures he had taken on the tour with his brand-new Nikon camera. There were literally hundreds and hundreds, and each one was more fascinating than the one before. I predict that Micky will really become a great photographer one day. With all his joking around, he is quite deep and serious and sees much more through the camera lens than we "ordinary" people see with our eyes.

CO-PILOT NESMITH

As I told you last month we were flown on the tour in our own private DC-6—and the flight from Dallas to Houston was unforgettable for one particular reason. Somewhere up in the air, about midway in our journey, Peter suddenly noticed that Mike was missing. "Hey, where's Nesmith?" he asked, jumping up from his seat (as you can see from the picture here, Peter has become a fanatic collector of beads, beads, *beads*). Anyway, we *all* knew where Mike was, but we weren't *about* to tell Peter—so we let him frantically search about for a while. When he couldn't find Mike anywhere in the passenger section of the plane, he stalked forward and threw open the cockpit door. There (to his surprise and dismay) sat his good friend Mike Nesmith at the controls of the airplane!

"Just take it easy, son," Mike said, in his best Texas accent, "Uncle Mike here is gonna look after biz-ness." Peter did one of his marvelous W. C. Fields "takes"—and lifting his eyebrows disdainfully, he walked slowly back to his seat and sat down!

There never seems to be enough space to tell about all the wonderful Monkee adventures I've been lucky enough to share. Right now, I'm back in L. A., working hard at my career as a singer, and hope to cut a hit record that you wonderful *16*-ers will really dig. Meanwhile, I'll do my best to keep an eye on those mighty busy Monkee-men of ours and, hopefully, I'll soon be telling you more, more, *more* about their magic Monkee world! 'Til then, stay cool. Luv ya'.

"Hey, where's Nesmith?!"

"Right here, son — takin' care o' biz-ness!"

MONKEES ARCHIVES 3

MONKEES ARCHIVES 3

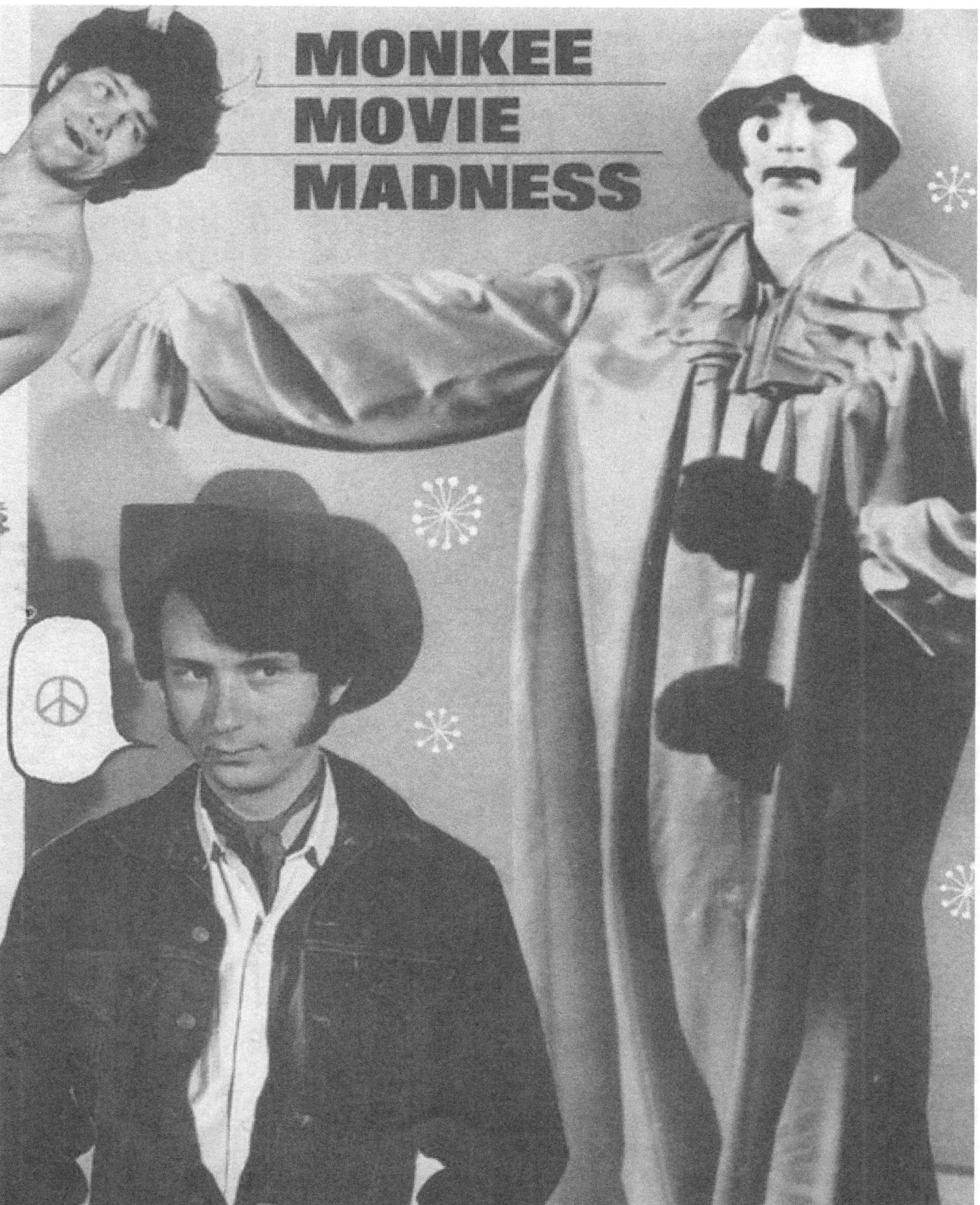

MONKEE MOVIE MADNESS

"MY DIARY OF DAVY JONES' EARLY DAYS!" By Linda Joyce Miller

Linda Joyce knew Davy when he lived in New York and was starring on Broadway in "Oliver!" They often saw one another, and Linda kept a diary of all these events. Now that Davy is one of the world's greatest super-stars, these early happenings take on a very special and important meaning. In this issue and in future issues of FLIP, Linda will share them with you.

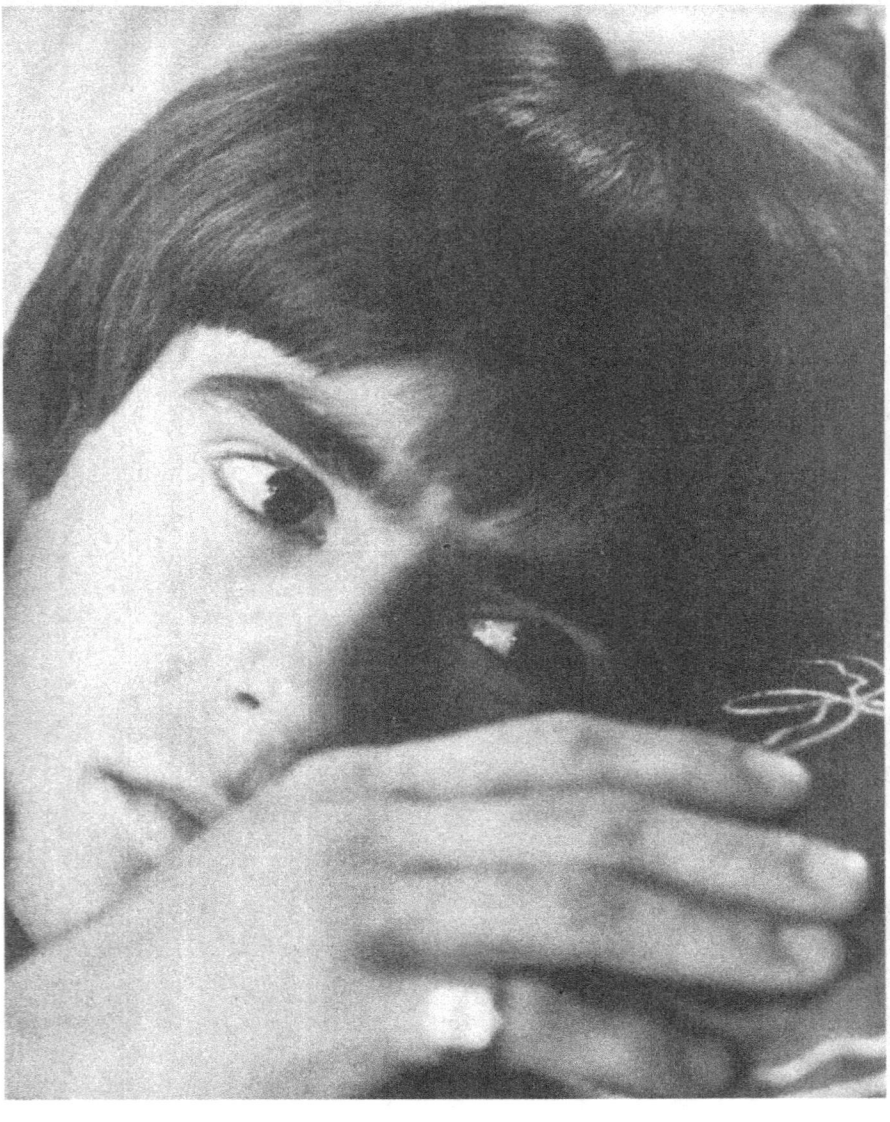

I've gotten a lot of letters asking why I always call Davy Jones DAVID when I write about him. When he was appearing on Broadway, he always asked to be called "David." If you had to call him DAVY, then he asked you to remember that it was D-a-v-E-y! The only ones I ever heard call him Davey were the small boys in "Oliver," who used to tease David by saying, "Hi, Davey, with an E!"

But when he became a Monkee, David Jones became Davy Jones. But I still refer to him in the way he preferred when I spent a great deal of time with him. And I have an idea that when he is no longer a Monkee, he will go back to calling himself DAVID JONES!

A lot of things about David have come to mind as I thought about this month's story. So, I thought the easiest thing to do would be to just kind of put them down as I think of them. Here goes...

1. He used to kiddingly refer to Jones Beach (in New York) as his beach.

2. David can talk perfect "New Yorkese," the American accent most New Yorkers have.

3. He used to cause traffic jams on West 46th Street in Manhattan by leading his fans on chases between all the cars and buses.

4. He doesn't like chocolate ice cream.

5. He loves vanilla ice cream.

6. David ALWAYS wore striped

MONKEES ARCHIVES 3

From Linda Joyce's collection of early photos of Davy comes this pic. Davy is wearing a striped shirt, as he always did when he lived in New York, standing outside of one of the coffee shops he used to snack at before and after the show with Linda.

shirts!

7. His dressing room number at the Imperial Theatre was 10.

8. In October, 1964, David had his appendix removed.

9. His favorite song then was "Any Old Iron," an English music hall song.

10. Some of the TV shows David was on before he became a Monkee were "Shindig," "Where The Action Is," "Ed Sullivan Show," "Ben Casey," and "The Farmer's Daughter."

11. Richard Burton was his favorite actor and "birdwatching" his hobby!

12. David was 16 when he came to America.

13. When he was 15, he played in a British touring version of "Peter Pan." His co-star, playing Wendy, was JANE ASHER.

14. When David became a Monkee, he must have thought back to October, 1964, when Jackie Cooper of Screen Gems said: "Every so often a youngster comes along with unusual talent and a capacity for professional growth which is practically a guarantee of stardom in all the entertainment media. In David Jones, we at Screen Gems feel we have a youngster who will soon be one of the nation's top all-around performers." Almost two years, to the day, later, David fulfilled that star-studded prediction!

15. David was nominated for a Tony Award (the Broadway version of the movie's Oscar Award) for his show-stopped performance in "Oliver!"

16. In England, David was on a radio program called "This Happy Land." His part was the longest radio part ever created for a teenager in British radio history!

It's happened again! I've run out of space for this issue. But I'll continue my memories of David in the next issue of FLIP. It will be on sale October 10th. See you then.

MONKEES ARCHIVES 3

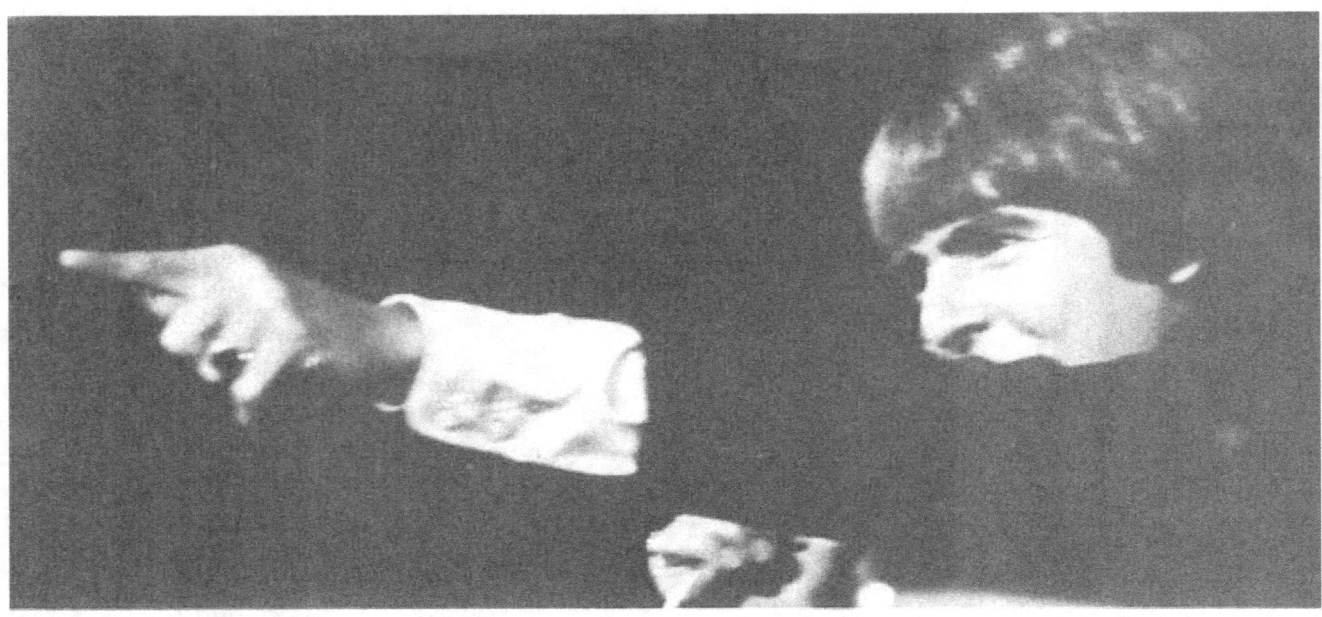

ON TOUR WITH THE MONKEES!

Have THE MONKEES come to your town yet?

This is what a visit by the fab four is like...

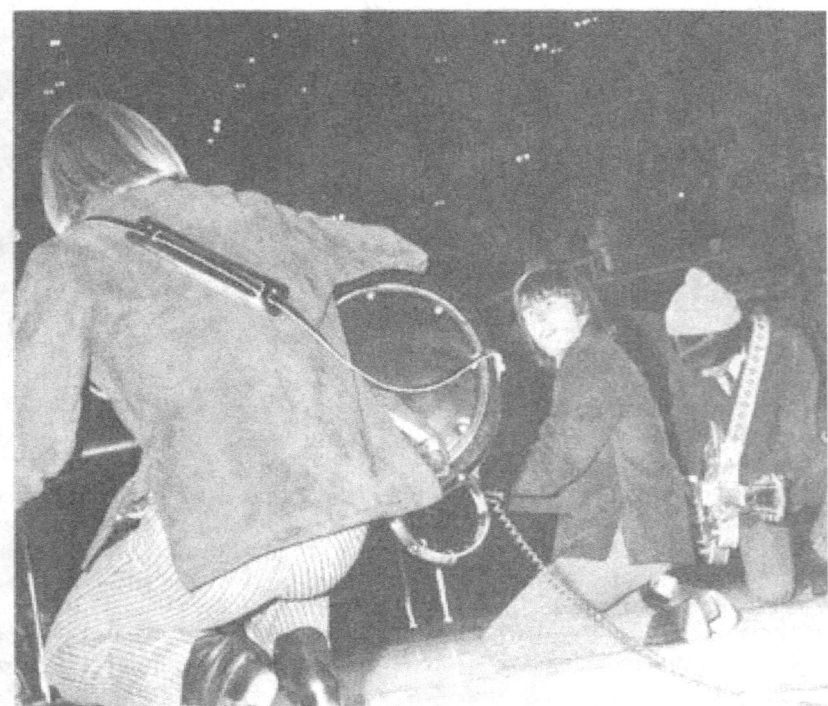

MONKEES ARCHIVES 3

Here, Davy and Micky check out the auditorium where they'll be performing that evening. Every stage has its own special problems, which The Monkees have to work out so that their spec sound doesn't change from city to city. If this groovy tour didn't convince everyone that each of The Monkees plays their own instruments, then nothing ever will!

ON TOUR WITH THE MONKEES!

Photos by Greg Gaston

The biggest problem for the guys is coming and going — without getting hurt. In each city, at every show, The Monkees have to scramble for safety. Here, Davy and Micky get ready to rush backstage. Peter, traveling in a second car, can be seen in the background.

Doing two things at once, Mike works on another mike while giving the crowd a quick once-over. Both the microphone and the crowd flipped for Mike!

Breathless and sweating, Peter pauses for a second on-stage, ready to give the crowd even more madness and music! If you've been lucky enough to see it, you know what kind of a great and groovy show they put on!

MONKEES ARCHIVES 3

Responding to the crowd, Micky grabs the microphone off the stand and flips out with another song!

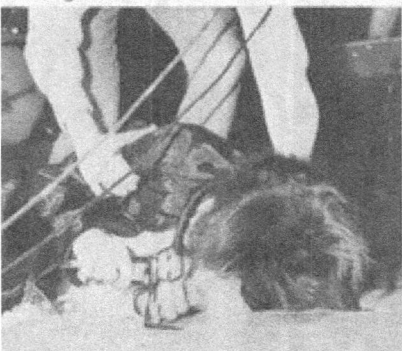

Micky gets carried away and gives it everything he's got!

This is what it would look like if you were on stage with The Monkees!

Micky getting ready for the action!

Tambourine in hand, Davy swings out . . .

In a different get-up, Davy keeps go-go-going! Which is really what Davy, Mike, Micky and Peter have been doing all summer!

TRAVEL WITH THE MONKEES! FLIP TO PAGE 62 FOR ANOTHER EXCLUSIVE OF THE MONKEES ON TOUR!

MONKEES ARCHIVES 3

MONKEE REFLECTIONS -- PART THREE
MIKE: "A Private Person!"

(The Monkees have been with us for nearly two super-years now. A lot has happened to them—and to all of us—during that period. We asked Carol Deck, FLIP's Hollywood Editor, who has been close to the group, to tell us how each of them has changed, if at all, during these twenty-three months. This is the second and final part of her report. Last month Carol talked about Peter and Micky.)

When the Monkees first began to happen Mike was the one who stood out the least and whom the least was known about. The first things anyone knew of him was that he was a Texan, a former folk singer and a married man. He seemed to stay in the background as the personalities of the other three became more and more public and this was the way he preferred it.

It wasn't that there wasn't much to him; it was just that he was, and still is a very private person who saw no reason for letting everyone in on what was going on in his mind, his home or his life. In this respect Mike Nesmith has not changed. He still is a Texan, a former folk singer, a married man and a very private person.

But then a public image for Mike began to emerge. At first it was often a comparison to John Lennon—he was the only one in the group that was married, his humor seemed to be rather on the sly side, he seemed as though he might be the intellect of the group, and it was rumored he was writing a book.

He eventually overcame the John Lennon comparisons and developed into his own public personality. People got to know Mike—tall and thin, slow talking, long thinking, devoted to his family and their privacy, a good guitarist, perhaps the best musician in the group, and a man with a bit of a temper when he feels he's being imposed on.

But there is one part of the image of Mike Nesmith that irritates Mike today. "I have a reputation for being sullen," he told FLIP, "And

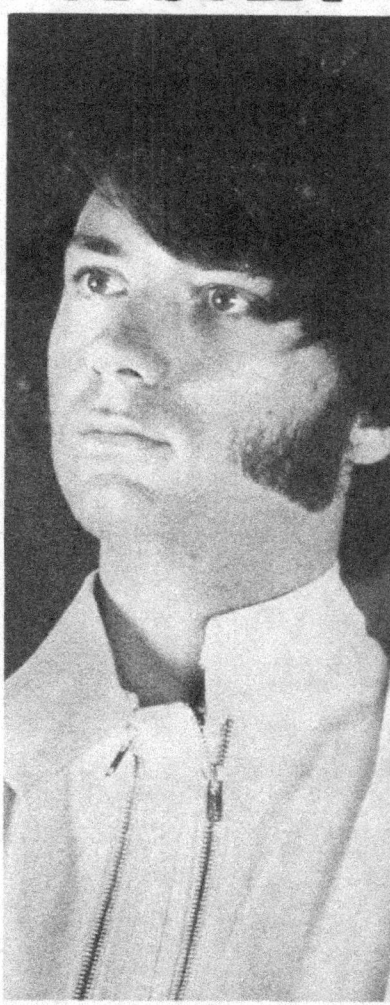

what I don't understand is why gentle men are always considered sullen."

And Mike is indeed a gentle man—perhaps he is also sullen sometimes. His humor may be one reason for the sullen tag. He becomes irritated when expected to be clever and witty 24 hours a day and slips into a humor that is often harsh, sometimes even crude, in defense.

He is also quiet and quietness is often mistaken for sullenness. When he has nothing to say, he doesn't small talk just to fill in the time. He simply shuts up. It is not that he is angry or speechless; he merely feels there is nothing to be said.

This is Mike Nesmith 1968—a young man who loves and is loved by a wife and two children, a musician who seeks to try new things and combinations of old things, an actor who idolizes W.C. Fields, a Southerner with the gracious manners and basic respect for femininity typical of the American South, a member of the now generation who believes that peace and love are the answers and that war solves nothing, a complete human being with thoughts and feelings like anyone else but with a certain something that makes him stand out above others—Mike Nesmith, a member of the Monkees.

MONKEES ARCHIVES 3

NEW COLGEMS SOUNDTRACK ALBUM SELLS THE MONKEES AND 'HEAD'

RCA Victor is putting a national promotion campaign behind The Monkees' best-selling albums and singles and their newest, the Colgems soundtrack album from "Head". Local showmen are urged to work closely with their RCA Victor distributor of this Colgems album!

THE MONKEES' RECORD OF RECORD HITS!

MONKEES ALBUMS	MOTION PICTURE	OTHER MONKEES SINGLES
The Monkees	"Head" (Soundtrack Album)	The Last Train to Clarksville
More of the Monkees	"Porpoise Song" (Single with flip side "As We Go Along")	I'm a Believer
The Monkees Headquarters		Pleasant Valley Sunday
Pisces, Aquarius, Capricorn & Jones, Ltd.		Daydream Believer
The Birds, the Bees and the Monkees		Valleri
		D. W. Washburn

Their RCA Victor records, on the Colgems label, would be enough to make The Monkees the reigning swing quartet of a swinging generation. But they also are international entertainment favorites as the result of their spectacular TV series, and their personal appearance tours. Now "Head" brings The Monkees to your screen!

- Provide posters and stills from "Head" for music store window displays and play Monkees records on theatre p.a.
- In addition to the AM and FM stations across the country, the "Head" album was serviced to all college and underground stations and it was given a big "push" in juke boxes.
- All local disc jockeys should have the new "Head" recordings as well as earlier discs by The Monkees. Suggest a "Monkees Mania" night or program during which their records are played exclusively, as a salute to their first film.
- Have distributor provide a quantity of records to be used as prizes, for presentation to libraries, VIP's and as giveaways.
- See that juke boxes in town feature The Monkee records with appropriate picture credits on the title labels. If possible, promote a juke box for the theatre lobby, offering free plays.
- Every community has vocal groups who entertain locally, either professionally or at parties, for their own amusement. With the cooperation of a local disc jockey, set a "Monkees Rivals" contest, in which the groups compete for promoted prizes, either on an air show or the theatre stage, with the deejay as M.C.
- The soundtrack album has a silver nylon cover which makes it particularly valuable as a display piece—in your lobby, in store windows, on walls, etc! Other albums covers, below.

RCA VICTOR RECORD DISTRIBUTORS

RTA Distributors, Inc., 991 Broadway	Albany, N.Y. 12204
RCA Victor Distributing Corp., 1500 Marietta Blvd., N.W.	Atlanta, Ga. 30302
Interstate Distributing Company, 457 Daniels	Billings, Mont. 59102
Eastco, Inc., 620 Memorial Drive	Cambridge, Mass. 02139
Southern Radio Corp., 1625 W. Morehead St.	Charlotte, N.C. 28208
D & H Distributing Co., 2500 Schuster Dr.	Cheverly, Md. 20781
Ohio Appliances, Inc., 7624 Reinhold Drive	Cincinnati, Ohio 45237
Main Line Cleveland, Inc., 1260 East 38th St.	Cleveland, Ohio 44114
CALECTRON, 460 Talbert Ave.	Daly City, Calif. 94014
Adleta Company, Inc., 1914 Cedar Springs Ave.	Dallas, Texas 75201
Ward Terry & Company, Box 869	Denver, Colo. 80201
Sea Coast Appliance Distributors, P.O. Box 546	Hialeah, Fla. 33011
Radio-TV Corp., RCA Victor Record Dept., 432 Keawe St.	Honolulu, Hawaii 96813
Art Jones & Company, Inc., P.O. Box 27	Houston, Texas 77001
Associated Distributors, Inc., 210 S. Meridian St.	Indianapolis, Ind. 46225
McClung Appliances, P.O. Box 3266	Knoxville, Tenn. 37917
RCA Victor Distributing Corp., 6051 Telegraph Rd.	Los Angeles, Calif. 90022
McDonald Brothers Company, Inc., 994 South Bellevue	Memphis, Tenn. 38102
Taylor Electric Co., 4080 No. Port Washington Rd.	Milwaukee, Wis. 53212
Heilicher Bros., Inc., 7600 Wayzata Blvd.	Minneapolis, Minn. 55426
McDonald Sales Corp., 5500 Jefferson Highway	New Orleans, La 70123
Bruno - New York, Inc., 460 West 34th St.	New York, N.Y. 10001
Krich - New Jersey, Inc., 428 Elizabeth Ave.	Newark, N.J. 07112
Dulaney's, 100 N.W. 44th St.	Oklahoma City, Okla. 73118
Sidles Company, 7302 Pacific St.	Omaha, Neb. 68114
Raymond Rosen & Co., Inc., 5Ft St. & Parkside Ave.	Philadelphia, Pa. 19131
Hamburg Brothers, Inc., Office Building, 24th & A.V.R.R.	Pittsburgh, Pa. 15222
Commercial Distributors, 50 Diamond St.	Portland, Me. 04101
North Pacific Supply Co., Inc., 2950 N.W. 29th Ave.	Portland, Ore. 97210
Huish Distributing Co., 2525 S. 8th W, P.O. Box 15038	Salt Lake City, Utah 84115
Fidelity Northwest, Inc., 5301 Shilshole Ave.	Seattle, Wash. 98107
Interstate Supply Co., Record Division, 2218 S. Jefferson St.	St. Louis, Mo. 63104
Morris Distributing Co., 1153 W. Fayette St.	Syracuse, N.Y. 13201
RCA Distributing Corp., Old Santa Fe Trail, 102 St.	Shawnee Mission, Kans. 66215
RCA Distributing Corp., 2700 Trolley Drive	Taylor, Mich. 48180

Half-Hour Interview Disc! Special Sleeve Tells What It's About. Order FREE From: Dick Strout, Inc. P.O. Box 907 Beverly Hills, Calif.

Dealer Co-op Ad Mat! One of Several "Head" Album Ads Distributed By RCA Victor (Shown Here in Reduced Size)

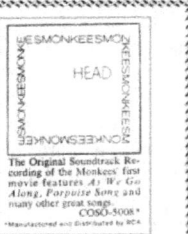

MONKEES ARCHIVES 3

MONKEES ARCHIVES 3

IN EXCLUSIVE:
The Monkees' Mike Nesmith Tells You All About:
"OUR INCREDIBLE LONDON HOLIDAY WITH THE BEATLES!"

Talk about fabulous vacations! There's never been one to equal Mike and Phyllis' trip to England to visit with The Beatles! And we have all the details... as told to Marcia Borie

Have you ever wondered what it's like to see London for the first time? Does just the thought make you tingle all over? Well, since we already assume that the answer to the first two questions is a resounding YES, here are a few more questions to contemplate...

Have you ever wondered what it would be like being one of The Monkees? Can you imagine how it would feel being married to a Monkee? And, assuming you were Mrs. Mike Nesmith on your first trip to England with your husband, can you imagine what it would be like to have the whole town at your feet AND to be the house guests of Cynthia and John Lennon?

Have you stopped swooning? Well, compose yourself. In fact, you'd better cool it, because you're about to hear the answers to all these spine-tingling questions!

It was still winter in London when Mike and Phyllis found themselves winging their way across the seas for a brief stay in England. The Monkees were already a sensation there. Pictures of the boys were harder to get than a mini-skirt reduced to half price. Their records were selling like fish and chips, and their fame was swinging like that "pendulum do...."

When Mike and Phyllis told me about their trip, they had already started to unpack, but they were both still up in the air!

Mike started first: "It was really so

Monkees' LONDON HOLIDAY

marvelous.... Fabulous is a better word. In fact, as much as Phyllis and I looked forward to the trip, I don't think either one of us ever dreamed how exciting and memorable a holiday it was going to be....

"I must admit, if you visit London for the first time—or for the fiftieth time—there's nothing like seeing it the way we did! First of all, we stayed in the city for a few days and that was just great. Phyllis and I walked up and down the streets, looking into shop windows, just gazing around at everything and trying to see as much as we could. It wasn't exactly easy to get around, on our own, I mean, but we managed....

"Then, John Lennon loaned us a fabulous car. It's a big black-curtained Princess, and we were driven around by his chauffeur, Alf. He took us everywhere we wanted to go, and since we didn't know many places, we just let him drive while we looked out the windows and stared. Then, when we went out to the Lennons' house in Surrey, we saw suburban life. Even being there such a short time, we did experience lots of contrasts.

"The English people are very nice.... *Really* nice! I mean, you know, let's face it, people in some of our States can be rude. *Actively rude!* The British are quiet and keep to themselves. They don't bother you. They don't intrude. Yet if you stop someone on the street and ask any question, they couldn't be more friendly or obliging."

"What I liked," Phyllis added, "was that tea. Everywhere we went, it was tea time. No matter what hour of the day or night people were always asking us to have a cup of tea. They certainly do have some lovely old traditions that they cling to.

"Everywhere we went we felt surrounded by a culture that's hundreds and hundreds of years old. It's funny in a way because London is so much connected with all the Mod influence. I think Mike and I really expected to see the whole town swinging, like that song says. But were really fascinated to find that actually they are about 40 years behind us in certain things.

"Mike says it's because they didn't go through the Roaring Twenties like we did. You can see it in their latest styles. The way the girls are bobbing their hair and wearing cloche hats. And, of course, the big rage is all those puffy fur coats. You dare not ask what kind of furs they are, because I don't think anyone knows! It seems the whole city is going through what we knew in America as the Flapper Era. It's kookie and fun—but it certainly isn't new."

Mike thought of something he'd neglected to mention, so once more he chimed in. "I can't begin to tell you how fantastic everyone was to us. I mean we were much more fussed over there than we are here. I've never seen so many photographers at one time.... And do you know that when we landed they had a headline in the paper that said: MIKE NESMITH ARRIVES. It was fantastic. Matter of fact, I wanted to get a few copies of the newspapers to bring home. But wherever we went, they were sold out.

"The whole experience was phenomenal. I can't remember when we've ever had such a marvelous time. As a matter of fact, we fell in love with London. I'll let you in on a secret—if there weren't a Los Angeles, Phyllis and I would want to live in London permanently. But as much as we lost our hearts to England, we still have to agree that, for us, there's nothing like L.A.

"Incidentally, our vacation was also very musical—in several ways. I mean, we visited many of the famous clubs in London and we really lucked out because there were some really great performers in town. While we were there, we saw the Stones, Jean Pitney, the Kinks, and Herman and the

MONKEES ARCHIVES 3

Hermits. We stopped at all the "In" places. Phyllis and I especially liked the Cromwell Inn. . . . And then we went out to stay with the Lennons, and that really was an unbelievably wonderful experience. . . .

"John and I established a great rapport. We were like kindred spirits. Believe me, it was really a great meeting of the minds—although I guess some people might think of a Beatle and a Monkee meeting as a crazy or funny event.

"Actually, John and I are just two guys who are doing what makes us happy, and being around each other was terribly stimulating. . . . He has a fabulous mind. I listened to him a great deal, and when I talked, he was not unimpressed. . . .

"It really was a marvelous experience for both Phyllis and I. She and Cynthia had as much rapport as John and I did. Frankly, right now John and Cynthia Lennon are about the only other couple in the world who Phyllis and I can be with and share the same experiences. . . .

"Also, it was very interesting to compare notes with John on a strictly professional level. Because I have written some of the Monkees' songs, and of course John and Paul McCartney have composed most of the Beatles' biggest hits, we launched into a marvelous conversation about composing, record sessions, and such things.

"John's also got a lot of great tape recording equipment at home that we fooled around with. I had a ball trying to learn how to play his Meletron. It's such a complex thing that it would take about a week to explain it. It's a keyboard instrument similar to a piano, but it makes all sorts of fantastic sounds that duplicate other instruments. . . ."

While Mike took a few breaths, Phyllis picked up the story.

"As wonderful as it all is, in a way it's sad for the boys. I mean, with both the Beatles and the Monkees, fame forces them to do one of two things—to perform, to face the public on stage, or to work in front of the cameras, and then to go home and hide behind their walls.

"The Beatles hide with their millions. In a way, they're really trapped. They just can't go anywhere. Why, do you know what John Lennon said to Mike? He said, 'Thank God for the Monkees, you've taken the heat off of us.'

"I must say Cynthia and I had a wonderful time being together while Mike and John were off talking. We cooked, and sat around, and traded stories about our babies. It really was such a calm, quiet, warm relationship that sprang up between us. They certainly are fine people. They made our stay in England so very memorable.

"Their home—I guess you'd call it very old English style—is big, several stories high. They have a lot of nice things, but the overall feeling is one of simple warmth and graciousness. It's done so tastefully—very subdued—the carpets and walls are dark and rich looking, and in a way quite traditional.

"Their living room reminded me of ours. I mean there were newspapers around. . . . Don't misunderstand, I don't mean it was messy. . . . It's just that their house looks lived in and very inviting. . . ."

Mike had caught his breath, and he wanted to add something at this point. "You know, it really is quite amazing how much the four of us are alike. We're all home-bodies. . . . Both John and I are devoted to our wives and feel the same way about our children. . . . Cynthia and Phyllis are both so warm and wonderful and down-to-earth. . . . Well, I know it sounds repetitious, but really I think we could have traveled the whole world and never have found two people so close to us—people who thought as we did, and lived as we did, who experienced what we did, and who felt as grateful as we did for all that's happened.

"You know, when I was with John, he represented to me the pinnacle of the kind of success that The Monkees are now beginning to enjoy. . . . When I saw how he was able to accept everything, and to remain so enthusiastic and productive, it really drew us closer together. They say that music is an international language. Well, I think the rapport between *musicians*, such as John and myself, is also something which knows no barriers. . . . John may have an English accent, and I may speak *(Continued on page 55)*

MONKEES

(continued from page 29)

with a trace of Texas in mine—but still, we speak the same language. . . ."

Both Phyllis and Mike promised to show me some of the fabulous Mod clothes they had brought back but had not yet fully unpacked. Meanwhile, we all agreed that the experience they had had was something that no amount of time could possibly erase.—THE END

WATCHING OVER HIS guests, Glen Campbell, loved working with the three zany Monkees. Mike and Glen got along great, because they both sing and write country-western music. Between shots they often sang together.

MONKEES ARCHIVES 3

You're under the sign of THE MONKEES "Pisces, Aquarius, Capricorn & Jones Ltd." ...and everything is favorable.

13 has just become a lucky number for you because that's how many songs The Monkees sing in their new album. The boys do "Pleasant Valley Sunday" as well as "She Hangs Out," "Words," "Daily Nightly," "Salesman," "The Door Into Summer," "Cuddly Toy," "Love Is Only Sleeping," "Star Collector" and "Don't Call On Me." Tune in to The Monkees tonight and turn on to the album tomorrow!

COLGEMS.
Manufactured and Distributed by RCA
Available on Stereo 8 Cartridge Tape

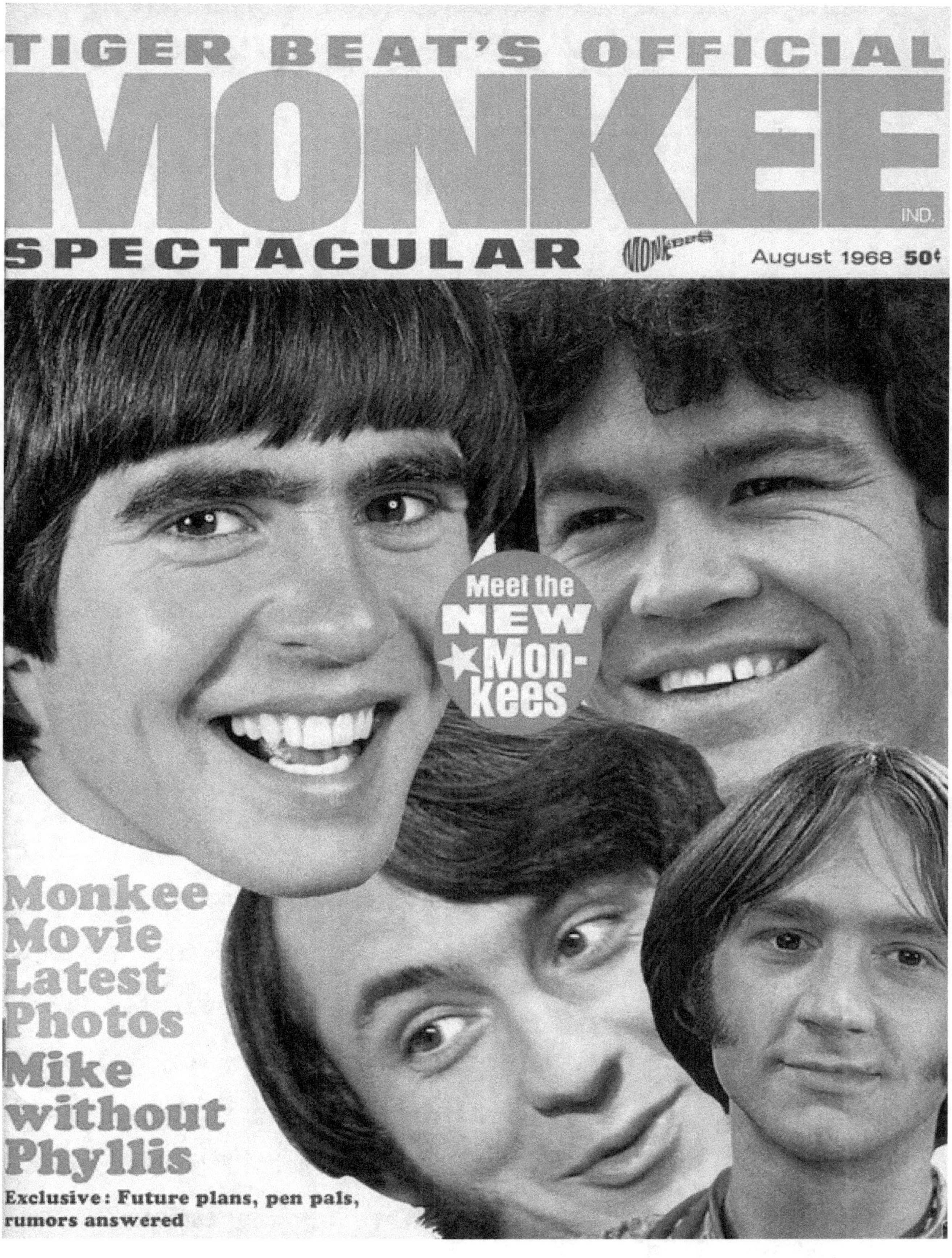

MONKEES ARCHIVES 3

TIGER BEAT'S OFFICIAL MONKEE SPECTACULAR

August 1968 50¢

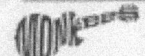

Meet the NEW Mon-kees

Monkee Movie Latest Photos Mike without Phyllis

Exclusive: Future plans, pen pals, rumors answered

MONKEES ARCHIVES 3

NOW P...
The Greatest...
starring DAVY JO...
MIKE NESMITH a...

Here we go again with some very groovy scenes from the Monkees' first movie. Hold your breath. It'll open near your town around Thanksgiving day and will be the wildest, funniest adventure in filming you've ever seen. It's still called "Untitled." Have any suggestions?

MONKEES ARCHIVES 3

...LAYING ...Movie Ever! ...NES, PETER TORK, ...nd MICKY DOLENZ

MONKEES ARCHIVES 3

ANNETTE FUNICELLO and DAVY play lovers in one segment of the film. That's Davy and his magic violin coming down the stairs at the right and the girl in the sailor suit is none other than Annette. How many of you remember the Mickey Mouse Club where Annette rose to fame?

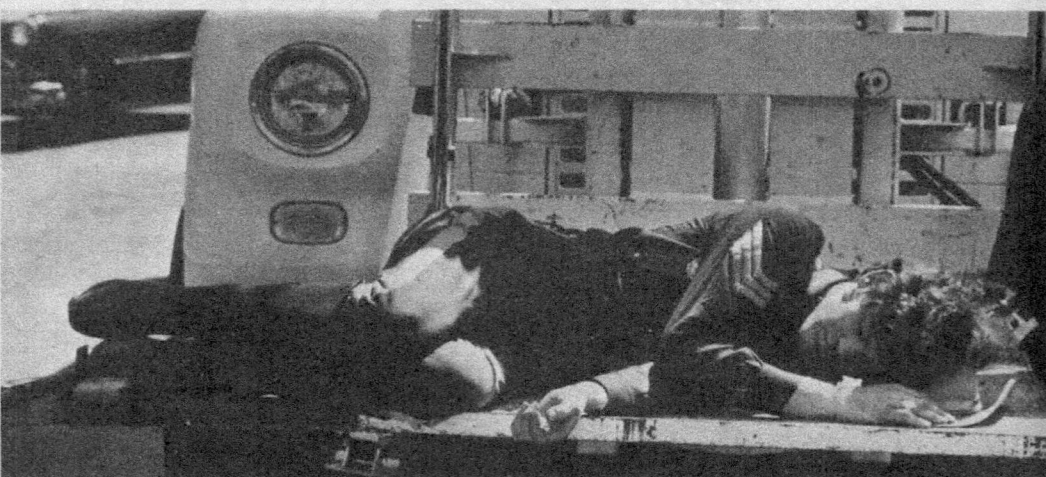

CLEVER MICKY catches a nap. Nope, this scene isn't in the movie. It's just Micky's way of getting some rest in between scenes. At far right he plays a Confederate Army officer in a segment of the film which does a takeoff on the Civil War movies.

MONKEES ARCHIVES 3

MONKEES ARCHIVES 3

MONKEES FLY! The boys filmed their flying sequences in a wind tunnel. They wore protective suits and Davy thought this was the most fun during the entire making of the film. Micky wasn't sure he liked it that much. Can you see the wires holding them up?

MONKEES ARCHIVES 3

MONKEES ARCHIVES 3

MONKEES SWIM! In one sequence all the Monkees had to jump in a swimming pool with their clothes on. That's Peter (right) in mid-aid before he hits the water. His moccasins shrunk from being in the water.

DAVY (right) contemplates movie making. This is Davy's first feature length film and he loved making it. Even if the Monkees don't do another feature in the next few years, Davy would like to squeeze one in on his own.

MONKEES ARCHIVES 3

ARE THE MONKEES SPLITTING UP?

If anyone told you—say, a year or two ago—that the fabulously successful *Beatles* would even dream of going their separate ways, you'd have every right to say, "It can't happen! After all, how

could they just pack up and walk away from one of the most glamorous careers in the history of show biz?"

Yet, you can see what's happening yourself to the Fab Foursome. *John* packed his makeup kit and took a starring role in a movie *without* his pals. He has always shown a greater interest in producing records and authoring books than in appearing with the group anyway. *Paul* has never made any bones about his preference for song writing. As for *Ringo*, he is already knee-deep in activities concerning his prosperous construction company. Not that the *Beatles* will no longer engage in any of their former joint efforts, but clearly, the team is not now—or ever will be again—the way it was! In short, the impossible *has* happened!

Could it happen to the *Monkees* too?

To arrive at a complete answer, one would have to look into the varied reasons why it happened, in the first place, to the *Beatles*.

On the surface the *Beatles* seemed to love all the excitement and acclaim they generated on their world tours. But to people close to them, it has been known for a long time that they were getting very weary. They had now reached the point where they knew they would never again have to worry where their next "quid" was coming from. Their earnings had been wisely invested, and their early hungers were definitely a thing of the dead, dim past. Most of all, they knew that if they quit then and there, they'd never have to do another day's work in their lives. So much for the plus side.

On the negative side, the boys were definitely fed up with living in a glass bowl. "No one can believe what it's like," *Ringo* once said. He was referring to the fact that not one of the frantic foursome dared show his face in public without being mobbed

by adoring fans. "We spend most of our time inside four walls," *John* said at another time. "They live like wanted criminals, holed up, never daring to show their faces," declared a member of the *Beatle* retinue.

This is the chief reason given for the *Beatles'* desire to go their separate ways. But there is one other reason. It is one thing to make it big, as they have, as a group. But in each one flamed a wish to prove *himself!* Was *John* good enough to make it on his own? Was *Paul?* Was *George?* And *Ringo?* According to people very close to them, this was one question each simply *had* to know!

The final question now remains to be answered—will the day come when the *Monkees* feel the same way? Will *they* too, sooner or later, tire of all the adulation, of the wild attention from worshipful fans? Will they too feel the need for some privacy, to get away from all the commotion they generate wherever they go? And will they too feel the need to prove themselves as individual stars?

The question has no easy yes-or-no answer. Of course, there are parallels in the careers of both groups. For the most part, the *Monkee* lads leaped from relative obscurity and humble beginnings to fame and fortune, almost overnight. Like the *Beatles*, the *Monkees* seem to possess that magical ability to arouse wild enthusiasms in their fans.

Thus far, the boys seem to be eating it all up. They are still enjoying the first flush of fame. This is indicated in small ways. For example, it isn't generally known that the *Monkees* request that 30 to 40 fans be admitted to watch the filming of their sequences for their top-rated TV series. It *is* generally known that all of them get big kicks out of making a sudden appearance before a crowd of teenagers in a fab sportscar.

To this point, it may appear that the balance is weighted in favor of the *Monkees* following the same path as the *Beatles*. But we have saved the major difference for the last. We refer to an innate humbleness possessed by each

MONKEES ARCHIVES 3

member of the *Monkees* group — a quality the *Beatles* were never known for.

Take *Davy*. "I have no intention," he declares firmly, "of forgetting the people I left behind." He was referring, of course, to the grimy, industrial town of Manchester, England, where he was brought up. *Davy* can't forget those early days.

Take *Peter*. "I've had my full share of troubles," he says softly. He may have been referring to the many, many months he spent working in a thread factory before trying to make it as a folk singer.

Take *Mike*. He usually sits in silence during interviews. "*Mike* hates to talk to strangers," explained *Davy*. Is there a clue to *Mike*'s moroseness in the fact that after his parents were divorced and his mother re-married, he left home? *Mike* won't talk about that. But he tries to explain his moody silences: "I'm thankful I was picked for the *Monkees*. I kinda avoid talking out loud about my future. I just sit and think about it. That's kind of where I'm

MONKEES ARCHIVES 3

If you guys ever DID break up, I think I'd just DIE!

at."

Take *Micky*. "A couple of years ago, I tried to join the Marines. They wouldn't take me because of my poor eyesight. I was heartbroken at the time—you know, *another* failure. Now, I'm glad." *Micky* wants things to stay exactly the way they are right now.

Examine the separate statements of the boys, and you will probably come to the same conclusion that *TEAN BEAT* has: the *Monkees* are here to stay for some time! For which, their millions of fans will no doubt send up a fervent prayer of thanks!

MONKEES ARCHIVES 3

PETER'S BIG THRILL!

and here he tells you all about it in his own words

The things that happened to us in England were all so exciting and I'll be telling you about them soon, but the thing that knocked me out more than anything was meeting the Beatles. Following our concerts in England, we had a huge party in this club called the "Speakeasy."

The way it happened was—our office called the Beatles' office and said "our boys are having a party and we'd like to know if your boys would like to come." And their boys came. I walked in and Paul was already there and he knew me without being introduced and that was a thrill! I shook hands with Paul; and Jane Asher was with him and I met a fellow named Barry.

INDIAN CHANT

I never found out his last name, he just hangs around with the Beatles and sometimes he's like a lightman and he does colors. He helps design shirts and he's an artist in the same outfit that designed the Hollies' album cover. They help design psychedelic stage shows.

A little after I met Paul, John and George came barreling in! They were wailing and screaming at the top of their lungs "Harekrishna." Harekrishna is an Indian chant. It goes, "Harekrishna, harekrishna, krishna, krishna, hare, hare, hare roma, hare roma, roma, roma, roma, hare, hare...harekrishna roma." George was playing a little banjo ukulele and it was painted really colorfully. They were all wearing their fab, neato, jet, gear.. all very groovy.

POUNDING TABLES

So we were all at the "Speakeasy" and there were records playing and a live group too. We didn't talk much, we mostly pounded the tables in time with the music and had a ball!

Lots of interesting things happened at the party. Paul went to leave the room, but there was no other way out, so he started to walk across the table and John said that Paul had no respect jokingly and Paul nodded. It was really funny, I thought I'd relate that to all the Beatle fans.

While the rest of us were banging tables, Paul picked up two ash trays and was shuffling them together and it made a great sound! We weren't singing at all, we were just keeping time to other people's music. Then sometimes we would go off on our own tangent and people would change the record, but we were interested in the earlier record and we'd keep right on beating in time to the first one.

GEORGE'S HOUSE

George said, "After this, we should go to my house and carry on." That didn't come to pass, because we broke up and went in different directions. I called George up a day or two later at his office and they said they would have George call me. So George tried to call me at my hotel and would you believe the operator wouldn't put him through!

Well, we finally got in touch and I went out to his house. The house itself is being painted by George's friends in all kinds of colors and designs. His mini cooper is painted bright yellow with some little designs on it.

RINGO, MO AND ZAK

We went out to visit Ringo at his house and I briefly met his wife and baby, only the baby isn't such a baby anymore. We went upstairs and there was a fellow standing there painting Ringo's mantel on the fireplace. All the Beatles are having great fun freaking out with the symbolism and the art and the designs on the walls. We listened to the radio for a while at Ringo's, but we didn't stay long, only about an hour.

After that, we went back to George's and had a meal. I think he's a vegetarian, because all we had for supper was vegetables. They were very good, though. Patti is beautiful and so sweet. Their house is very simple considering...it's roomy with lots of windows. I saw George's sitar and we talked a bit and then he played for a bit.

SIMILAR PHILOSOPHIES

We spent a lot of time discussing getting it all done. Getting all what done? I'm not quite sure. I think it's what's happening—all you need is love and baby you're a rich man. Those aren't titles, those are phrases. Those are statements, and they're true—baby, you're a rich man, you keep all your money in a big brown bag inside a zoo, and you're a rich man. Anybody can do it, maybe I'll write a song to that effect. You can do it, it's just a question of getting everybody to believe.

Our ideas about this life are very much alike—almost totally. George is very influenced by the Eastern Indian thing, mainly because the Eastern people have a larger grasp of what he's interested in. I also have some of these interests and it was a fantastic experience sharing them with George.

The Monkee Show

You've got to understand how it all works on the Monkee stage: first of all there is the director, Jim Frawley, and he is like the captain. What he says goes. He orders the whole troupe into action. Then there is Jon Anderson, the assistant director. He is like the first mate. Before the hubbub and carrying on can be really put down, Jon Anderson has to make sure the director is ready to shoot the scene, make sure the boys are on the set ready to shoot, make sure the cameraman, Irving Lippman, is ready to put his crew into action.

Then Jon Anderson yells "Quiet" at the top of his voice. And he means business. When he yells, there really is quiet on the set. Grips stop in their tracks, the hairdresser halts in her ministrations to the pretty head of the guest star, guests try to breathe even quieter, and then Jon Anderson says "Roll 'em."

The camera operator says "Speed" when the big Mitchell is running smoothly, and the sound mixer seated at his console says "73" or "one hundred and four" or whatever shot number it is, and then Jim Frawley leans forward watching the boys intently and says like the crack of a whip: "Action."

Camera in Motion

And then Micky moves toward the door of the pad, and Davy moves with him, the camera follows them, then Peter and Mike enter the area in front of the lense. Slowly the scene unfolds and all too quickly Jim Frawley yells "Cut." Most of the time he also yells "Print." And that means that the boys have done a good job and the scene will be printed and shown to the producers tomorrow. If something isn't just quite right and he wants to shoot

MONKEES ARCHIVES 3

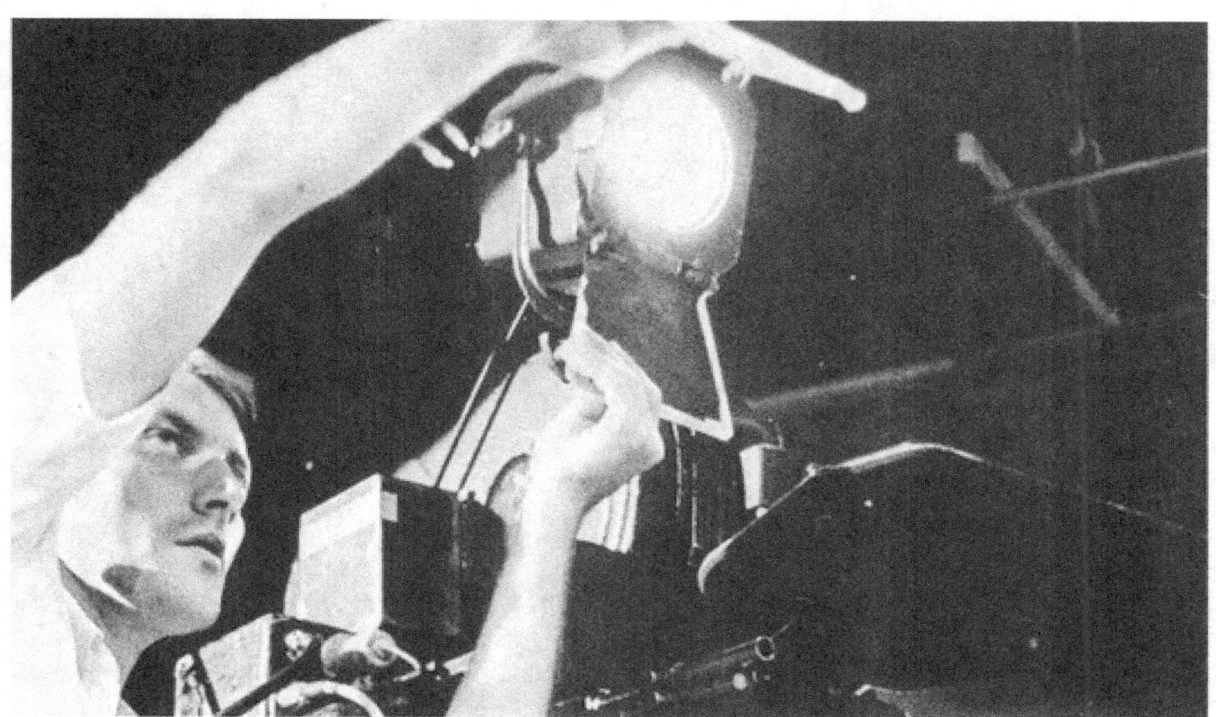

w: How it Works!

MONKEES ARCHIVES 3

it again he'll walk out in front of the camera and gather the boys around him.

"Micky," he'll say, in a for instance situation, "Micky, remember that you don't like this guy, and you've got to get his attention away from the other guys so they can circle around back of him. Act like you were really scared of him. Right?"

"Got it, babe," Micky will probably say, and then Jon Anderson will get a nod from Jim and he'll yell "Places everybody. Let's do it again, Quiet!" And the routine starts all over again.

The routine is usually hard and tiring on television shows, but on the Monkees' set it's kind of different. Here are the four top names in the entertainment business doing their scenes for one of NBC's hottest television shows. Obviously this makes the operation a little special. The police officer sitting quietly over there by the stage door isn't an ordinary part of a television crew. But this is the "Monkees."

This is the famous Stage Seven. There's a lot of tradition around this crew, after only a year of being a team. Being part of a hit show makes a team proud of their show, and when everyone is as friendly and close as they are on Stage Seven, a "family" feeling develops. Part of it derives from the fact that the Monkee crew works faster and prints more takes in a day than any other crew on the lot. They're mostly young, younger than any crew in Hollywood, and they're all eager to do their very best for the boys. Everyone is on a first name basis with everyone else, and at times the boys have been home to dinner with families of the crew, and vice versa. It provides a background of friendship among the cast and crew hard to equal except maybe on the crew of a submarine. These men and women go through a lot of hard work together; no wonder they have so much fun together.

Now the camera is being moved into another part of the set, the boys are changing into still another set of costumes and the gaffer is lighting the new area where the director intends to shoot. Gene Ashman, the man who has charge of the Monkee wardrobe, is in the dressing room with Mick.

Tight Pants

"Babe, this'll never fit." Micky is getting into a tight pair of jeans.

"Stand up, Mick, I'll get 'em on you." Gene is charged with a huge responsibility, since he has not just one but four sets of costumes to worry about on the show. And the boys make many costume changes. Gene is hard-working and serious, takes no nonsense on the set, but he likes the boys and they like him. Micky stands up, Gene hauls; the pants go on.

"I'll never breathe again," Mick jumps around the room, getting used to the tight fit. A pretty girl walks in without knocking. "Hi," Micky scarcely notices her. The girl picks up a bunch of notes on the table by Micky's couch.

"I'll have the list for you, later," says the girl and walks out.

Micky does a take then says to Gene, "What list?"

Gene shrugs. The girl is from the Monkee front office. It's always a little hectic being a Monkee, and half the things that go on for the boys have to be planned and set up without even having a chance to tell the boys first. Their schedule is too tight to take time out for planning things. So they depend on the front office to handle it all. It works out well that way.

However, it means that the Monkees' lives are pre-planned for them most of the time, and it means that the boys are lucky to call a minute their own when they're not on vacation. It's a hectic schedule. That's the way Mick feels as he walks gingerly out of the dressing room wearing the tight pants, on his way once again to face the cameras.

MONKEES ARCHIVES 3

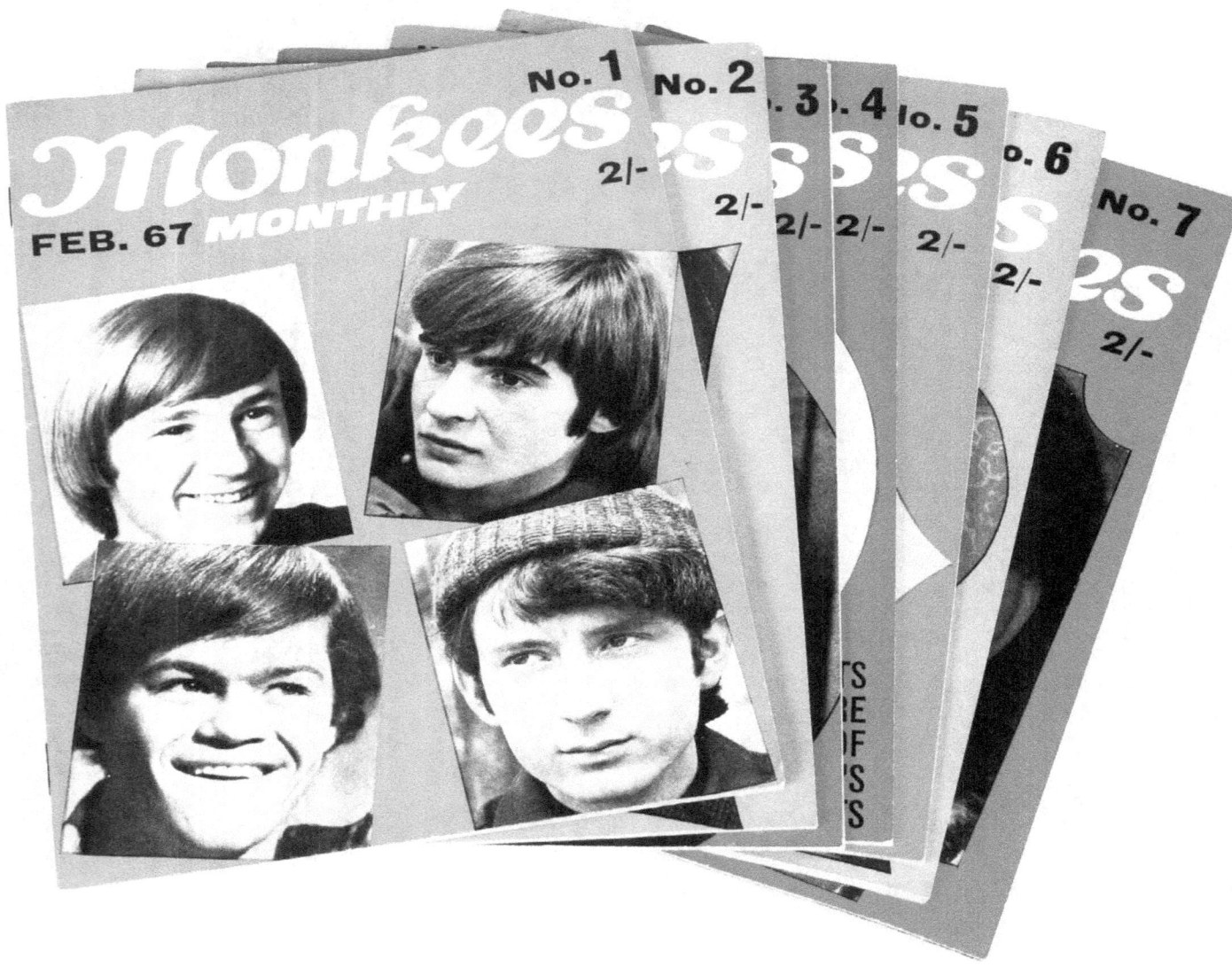

MONKEES ARCHIVES 3

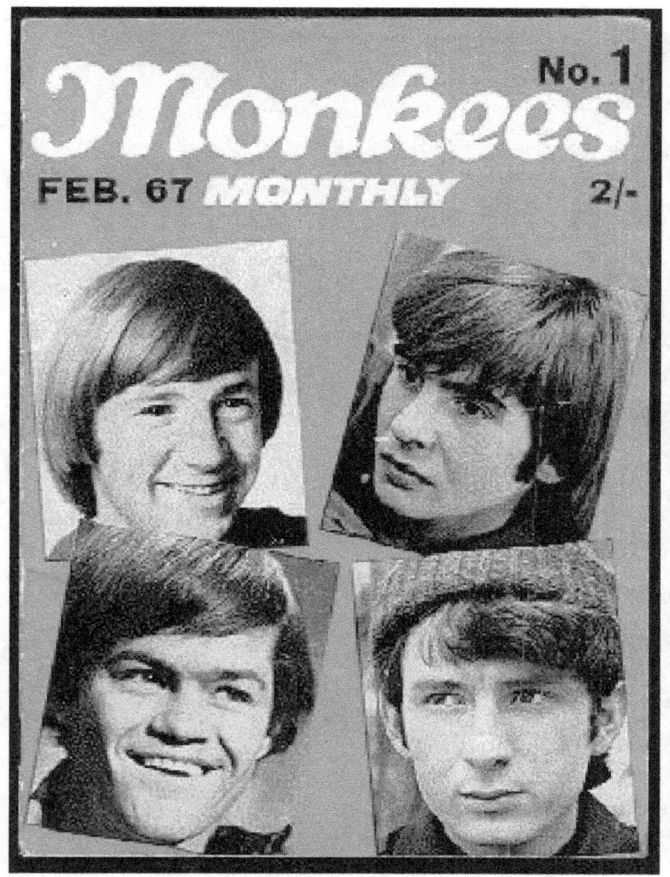

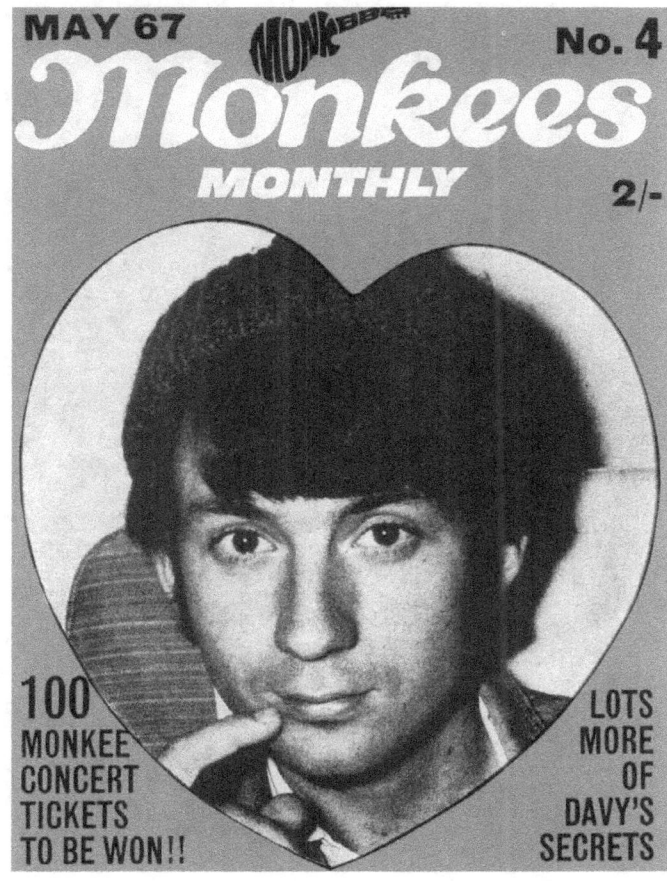

MONKEES ARCHIVES 3

MONKEES ARCHIVES 3

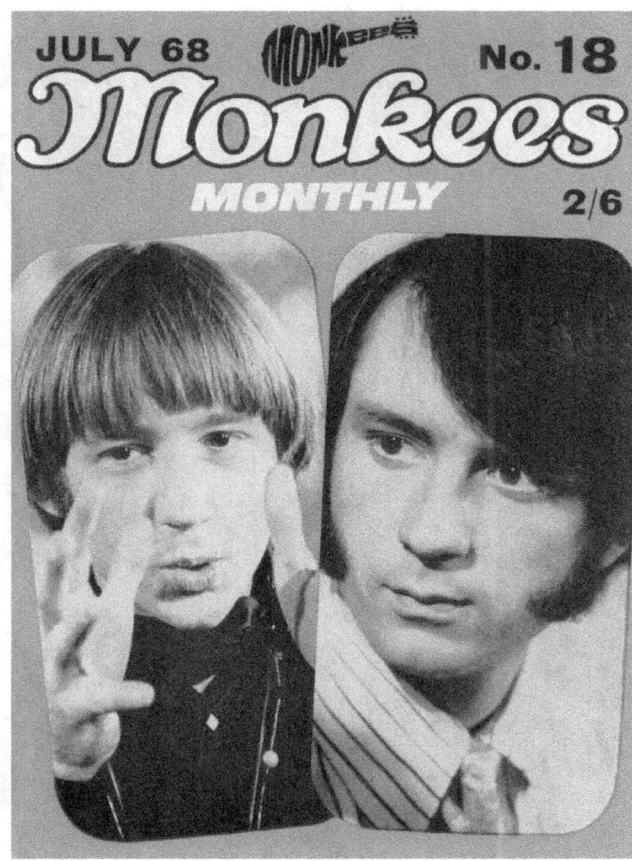

MONKEES ARCHIVES 3

MONKEES ARCHIVES 3

MONKEES ARCHIVES 3

MONKEES ARCHIVES 3

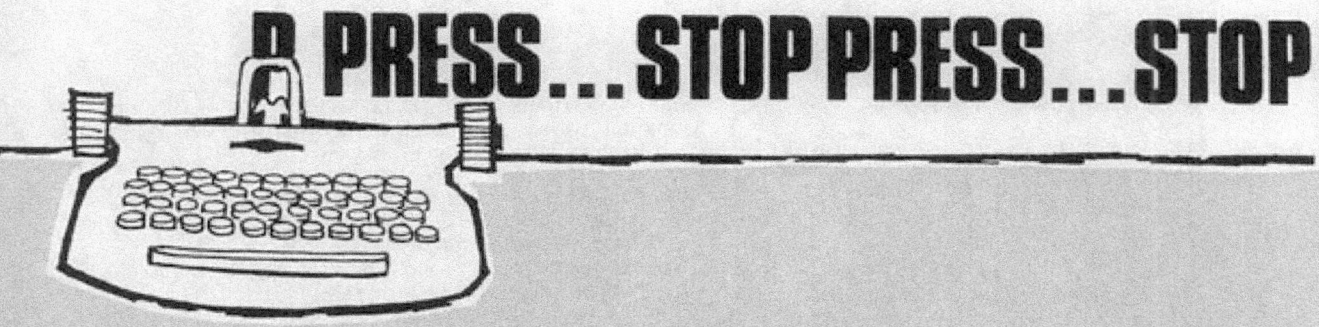
PRESS...STOP PRESS...STOP

SAMMY joins MICKY

Samantha Juste and Micky Dolenz are becoming inseparable these days. She flew out to California to visit Micky some weeks ago and also joined him in Paris a few days before the start of their British tour. After fulfilling some important engagements, she flew out of London Airport on Friday, July 14th to be with him on their current American tour.

Favourite Club

All the Monkees visited several of the "in" London clubs whilst they were here. Top of the list by the time they left, was definitely the Speakeasy, which is also the favourite haunt of top pop stars and musicians. It was the location for a big party which Nems gave for the Monkees, on Monday, July 3rd, with the Beatles, minus Ringo, as star guests.

RETURNING SOON

All the Monkees said that they were knocked out with the reception they received in England. Peter Tork commented: "Everything here seemed to be so much bigger than in the States. We can't wait to come back, not only to meet up again with all the friends we've made this time, but also to visit lots of the other cities in Gt. Britain. And we're going to try and make it again before the end of this year".

PETER AND MIKE COLLAPSE

Both Peter Tork and Mike Nesmith collapsed from exhaustion after the Sunday afternoon concert at the Empire Pool, Wembley. Mike, however, told me that it was just brought on by the heat and that after a few whiffs of oxygen he felt O.K. The Monkees' management were a bit worried as to whether the boys would be able to get through their seventy minute performance on Sunday evening, and before they went on stage, the Monkees went into a huddle, wishing each other the best of luck. The evening performance went off without incident, probably due to the cooler atmosphere, and towards the end they even inserted an extra song. Davy told us afterwards that they would have done several more if they could have got the audience to quieten down in order to tell them what was happening.

Immediately they returned to the States they started a hectic 28-show tour.

MOTOR CYCLE FAN

Micky seems to enjoy any dangerous sport. His latest hobby is motorcycle scrambling and he's often seen tearing up and down the hills behind his home in Laurel Canyon.

NEW AMERICAN SINGLE

A new Monkees' single was released in the States on July 14. The 'A' side is "Pleasant Valley Sunday", a Goffin & King composition. 'B' side is "Words". Both the tracks were recorded during the last big sessions before the Monkees' British tour, and were produced by Douglas Farthing Hatelid.

DID NOT FALL

Monkee fan Tina Ridgeon, of Battersea, London, was most annoyed to find that she had been reported in the papers as having jumped off the balcony at the Saturday concert, to try and reach the Monkees on stage. She phoned us after she had been released from hospital, to tell us that she had not jumped but was pushed from behind.

COMPLETE SONG-BY-SONG ACCOUNT OF THE WEMBLEY CONCERTS

Wembley Pool is a massive stadium. It seats 10,000, and every one of those seats shivered and shook on June 30, July 1 and 2, when the Monkees were in residence for their five concerts—five sell-out sensations, which just couldn't be beaten for excitement, production, scream-provoking brilliance... well, just call it a Parade of Talent.

We were there, backstage and in front. We noted that the boys never worked at less than one hundred per cent efficiency. They sometimes gave the impression of making things up as they went along, but really it was a wondrously-planned production in which everything fitted just right. Some fifty thousand fans were there over the three days. Maybe a million more couldn't make it. So as a souvenir for the first Lucky Lot and as a bit of compensation for the Miserable Million, here's what actually went on on that amplifier-littered stage.

SUPER-SMASHING

We're concentrating on that last super-smashing show on the Sunday night. But the dramas had started on the very first show. For the boys were late. The traffic had caused the trouble and it's the very first (and probably last!) time they've ever kept an audience waiting. It was left to Jimmy Savile, in his short-trousered pink and white suit, to keep things ticking over ... accompanied by his Frankenstein-Dummy "mate". He did well, especially coping with ten thousand throats all chanting "We Want The Monkees".

Behind the stage, on a lower level, was a canvas-screen dressing-room where the Monkees made their quick changes of costume. There wasn't time for them to nip round to their main Pool H.Q....

QUICK CHANGES

For speed, and quick changes were the essence of the whole thing. But let's dig deep into the last show of all. Starting with Peter Murray arriving on stage, in blue blazer and a sun-tan. He urges fans to take their seats... earlier in the interval he'd said: "If there's ANYTHING you want to do, do it now". There are adjustments to the blue-canvas tunnelling through which the boys will finally appear and bound on stage.

The excitement is unbearable; the suspense killing. The screams reach a crescendo. There's a sort of fanfare over the speakers. All eyes glued on the stage. And suddenly in a flurry of red velvet suits there they are. They cavort on stage and the noise is deafening. They go through a

MONKEES ARCHIVES 3

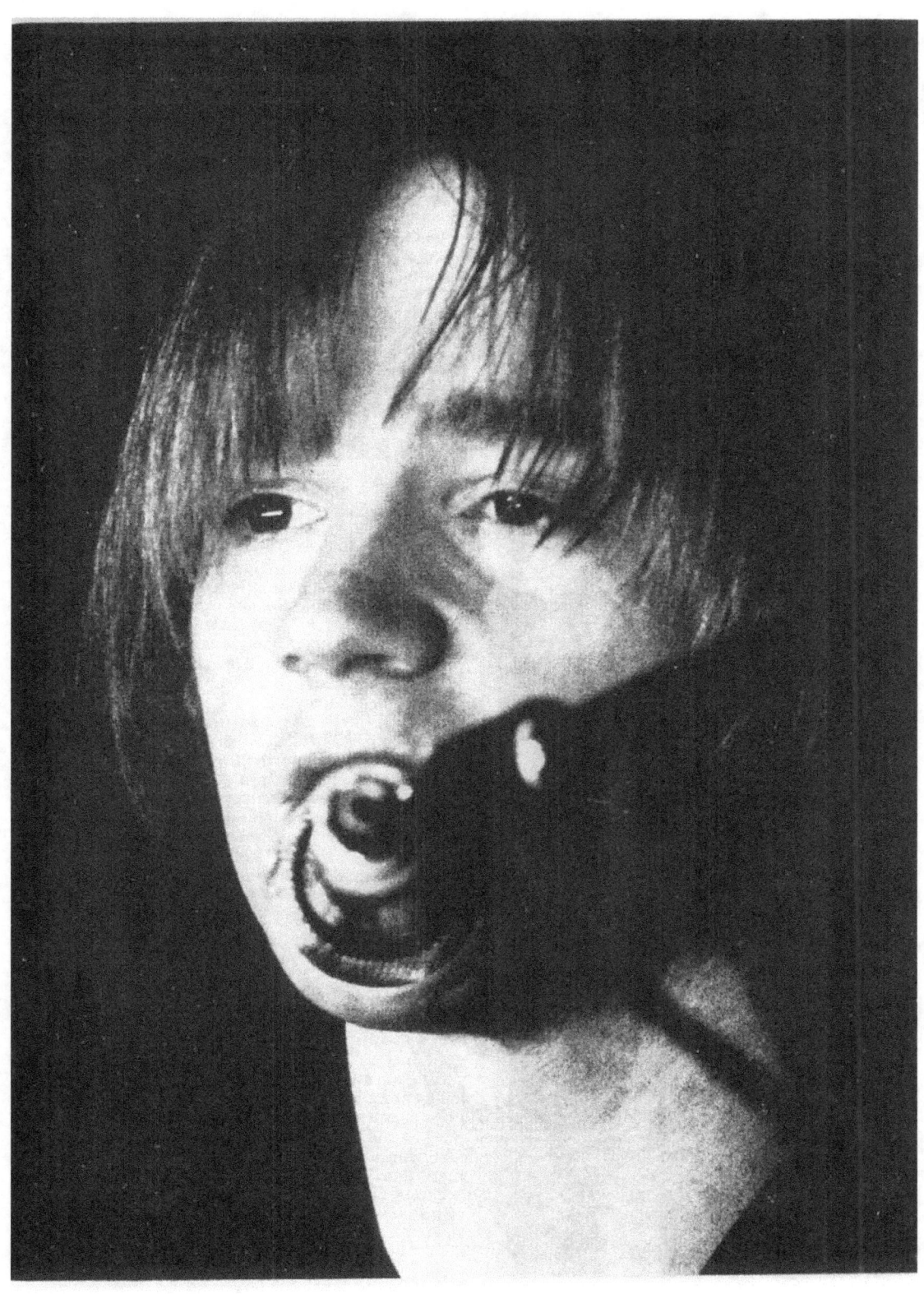

MONKEES ARCHIVES 3

little bit of informal tuning up, testing equipment. Mike gestures that one of the amplifiers is not quite right ... twiddles with a knob.

Above them is a massive projection screen. We wonder, at first, what that's all about. We soon find out.

And at a signal from Mike, the boys launch into their great "I'm A Believer". Davy has picked up Peter's bass guitar, plucking away happily. Peter is at the organ—he has a mini-piano near at hand too. Davy looks a little stern-faced right at the start. They look out at a sea of waving arms. Micky spares a thought for those behind the group on a built-up tier—blows kisses madly and energetically from behind his drums. Mike concentrates intensely on the neck of his guitar, smiling occasionally as the audience reaction builds to a new climax.

MESSAGES FROM FANS

A fantastic start. And into "Last Train To Clarksville". Davy throws his tambourine high in the air—fails to catch it. Explains to Micky, who laughs in sheer disbelief. Davy finds another tambourine. Davy, Micky and Peter sing ... and an attendant hands out cotton-wool for the sensitive ears of the photographers up near the stage. A shower of messages are thrown onto the stage by fans. Another Monkee hit powers to a finish. Mike steps forward for an announcement we can't hear. Peter flashes his widest grin. Davy tries to communicate with Mike by sign language.

And it's into "You Just May Be The One", Mike singing, Micky head-shaking so that his hair fluffs out more than usual. Mike ploughs on through this lovely number, left leg jerking to the beat. By now the cheering and the screaming and the response is almost uncontrollable. Same thing through a Sunday Night Special ... "Sunny Girl Friend" is added, Micky singing for this particular show.

PETER'S SOLO

Then a personal favourite of mine—"Auntie Grizelda". Peter singing most of the way, having ditched his guitar. Davy moves over to a piano-bass, playing booming notes with his right hand, left hand supporting him. Peter in fabulous form, swinging his arms, whipping up excitement, suddenly pointing—and suddenly getting a wave of screams from where he points. Wowee, we thought. How much longer can the boys keep this hectic pace going ...

Then the ultra-beautiful "I Wanna Be Free", featuring Davy. And the screen is used for the first time. As the lyrics are unfolded, to fantastic acclaim, colour slides are used, showing Davy on the beach, playing with children, on a horse

MONKEES ARCHIVES 3

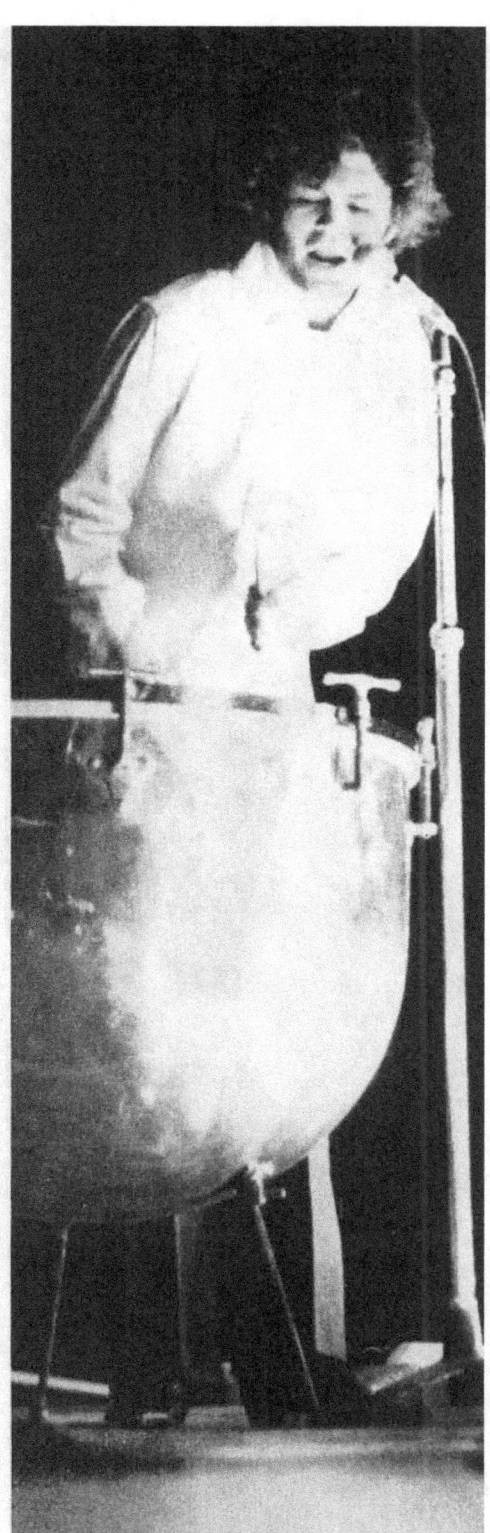

—a special slide of Mick Jagger is included, too. Davy clutches two mikes then, to fantastic screaming, slides down on his back on stage, out of sight of us in the front. His expressive face reveals the sincerity of his performance... a tiny figure, holding a massive audience in the palm of his hand. Peter moves back, out of Davy's personal spotlight. Shouts of "Davy, D-a-v-y-"... as the Jones boy coils in the mike lead and picks up tambourine again.

JUMPING DUET

Next it's "Sweet Young Thing", Mike singing, Micky grinding out a dramatic beat on snare drum and tom-tom, then Davy and Peter come in on the vocal. Peter and Davy jump up and down, athletically and together, like twin jack-in-the-boxes. Unbearable, now, the excitement. And on to a final curt "yeah" from Mike on the last notes, which triggers off an informal conference between Mike, Peter and Davy as screams, applause and cheers wash over them.

"Girl I Knew Somewhere" was no less effective. This up-tempo piece, with Peter on bass now and Davy on tambourine. The boys' white polo-neck sweaters contrasted with the red of their suits. On to a short thump of an instrumental finish, Davy looking a trifle anxiously at Mike as the last chord is struck.

On to "Mary, Mary", Davy retreating to the piano-bass again, with Peter on organ. Mike handling the main vocal line with his rather stern facial expression accenting his sheer concentration—and an ear-breaker of a scream when Davy flew to the centre for a few quick dance steps.

MIKE AND MICKY

And then the beat is continued as the boys prepare for their actual solo spots. Film extracts flash on to the big screen—the boys in top hats, in Stone Age gear. Davy on maraccas, waving wildly, then moving on to drums as Micky moves right forward to grab the mike. Davy and Peter go off stage, leaving Mike and Micky operating in a riot of comedy. Micky takes a photograph of the posturing Mike; then Mike grabs the camera. Then Mike photographs the photographers. Micky does his teeth-chattering bit, raising the roof. And off goes Mike, leaving Micky strutting around the stage, shouting "hello" and blowing kisses, a curious high-shouldered sort of ambling walk.

He introduces Peter's solo spot on "Banjo Cripple Creek". On comes Peter, in white woollen sweater, white slacks. Armed with his banjo. His left foot bounces in tempo as he shows astonishing skill on his Blue Grass-style banjo picking, singing too. Then a quick "thank-you"

MONKEES ARCHIVES 3

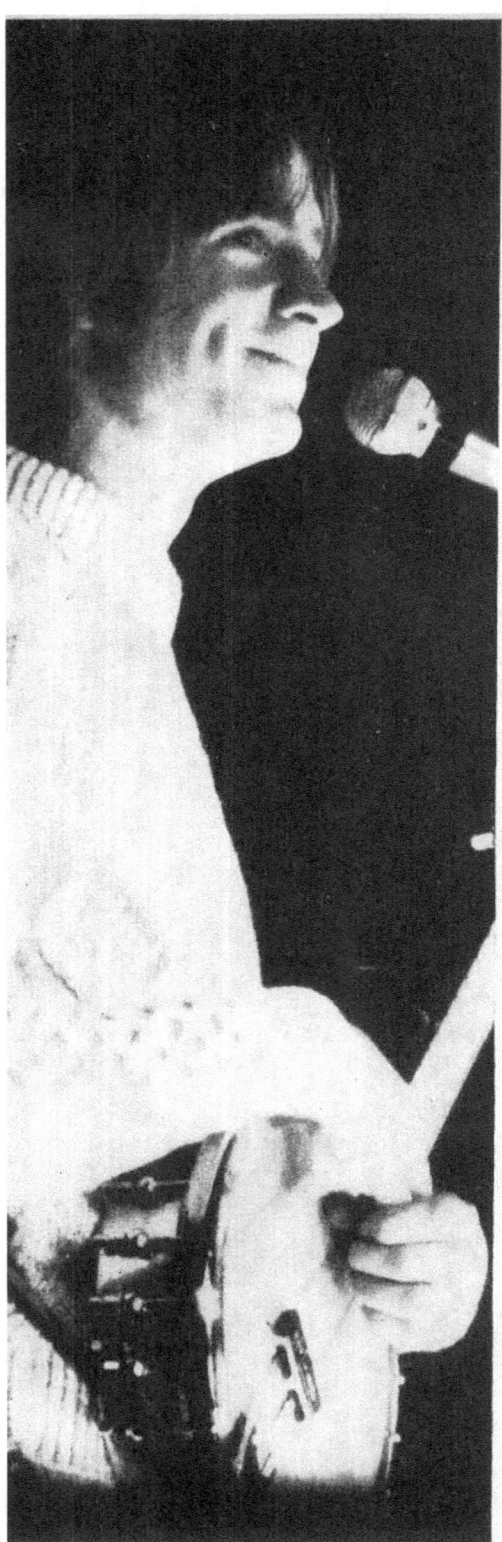

and he pretends to shut out the deafening screams by clapping his hands over his ears. And it's on to Mike's turn . . .

He wears a white-pleated jacket, electric blue trousers, open neck shirt. Grabs the microphone, plays a harmonica lead in to "Can't Judge A Book By It's Cover", later taking up three maraccas in each hand, shoulders flying as his whole body shakes. Wild blues, country-style. He goes into a Groucho Marx-type stooped walk across the stage. He plays to all parts of the audience. Then ends, coat flaring out, Mike hanging limply forward.

DAVY SINGS

And it's on to Davy, who sings "Gonna Build A Mountain". A grey-suited figure, bell-bottom trousers, little dance steps works in. His index finger leads in the members of the Echoes, who are providing the backing during the solo spots. He flings off his coat. Screams. He slides across the stage. He sinks to his knees. More screams. Hysteria now. Mike comes on, does a funny little dance routine with Davy, who vanishes from sight as Mike introduces Micky.

It's Micky "James Brown" Dolenz. He wears a brocaded white three-quarter length coat that he'd bought in London after the opening night. Striped black trousers. He postures round the stage, combing his hair. Flickering lights add to the effect. He sings "I Gotta Woman", a real wildie of a number. He flings off his coat, revealing an orange shirt. He flings himself around, sliding, hurling, jerking. On comes Mike, holding a black cape which he throws round the shoulders of the apparently exhausted Micky. Off they go, then Micky suddenly throws off the cape, slides back to the microphone and goes on singing. Again Mike puts the cape round Micky, again Micky chucks it off, this time somersaulting back to the microphone. One fan got through the guard of commissionaires, Micky reaching forward and touching her hand. Lucky girl!

EXTRA TIME

We've had the lot—music, singing, comedy, drama, everything. But as the hour shows up on the clock, there's still more. There's "Alternate Title", the boys returning on stage together (as the Echoes slip away), in white suits (double row of buttons) and orangy shirts. They sing, in ad-lib style, "Happy Birthday" to a fan-friend there in the front block. Mike tries to explain that they'll do more numbers if only the audience will let them be heard. Mike says, that he'd rather the main screaming came at the end of a song rather than during it.

Davy tries to get a bit of hush. No joy. Into their current hit, eventually. Davy singing,

MONKEES ARCHIVES 3

Peter on organ. Slides, in colour, flash with precision-timing on the screen. Davy sings specially for those there behind the boys. He kneels, then almost lies down. Everything raises the roof. He carries a tympani drum down to the centre of the stage and Micky comes down to hammer out short phrases on it—Davy literally smashing the cymbals on Micky's drum kit as the rhythm builds. A positive frenzy of noise, then, as Davy starts hammering the tympani, Micky retreats. This is surely it—the finish. The boys look tired . . . as well they might.

Yet there is still even more. They always close with "Stepping Stone", accompanied by another burst of colour slides—each one earning a separate cheer and scream. And this is where the stage really bursts into colour and visual excitement.

INCREDIBLE ENDING

Multi-coloured lights flicker and change. Davy on piano-bass, Mike crouched by the amplifiers, producing wailing guitar sounds. Davy ends with his maraccas. And the show ends with incredible excitement. Then, quite abruptly, it's a quick "Thank you" from the boys, they turn, waving and smiling then nip downstairs to make a fast getaway. In a rather dirty, old, blacked-out van.

But they left a lot behind. They left an exhausted audience, memories of the most staggering pop performance ever. The boys had worked unstintingly for more than seventy minutes. They'd given their all to please their knocked-out fans.

I'll never forget it. Never. Those Magnificent Monkees.

JACKIE RICHMOND

MONKEES ARCHIVES 3

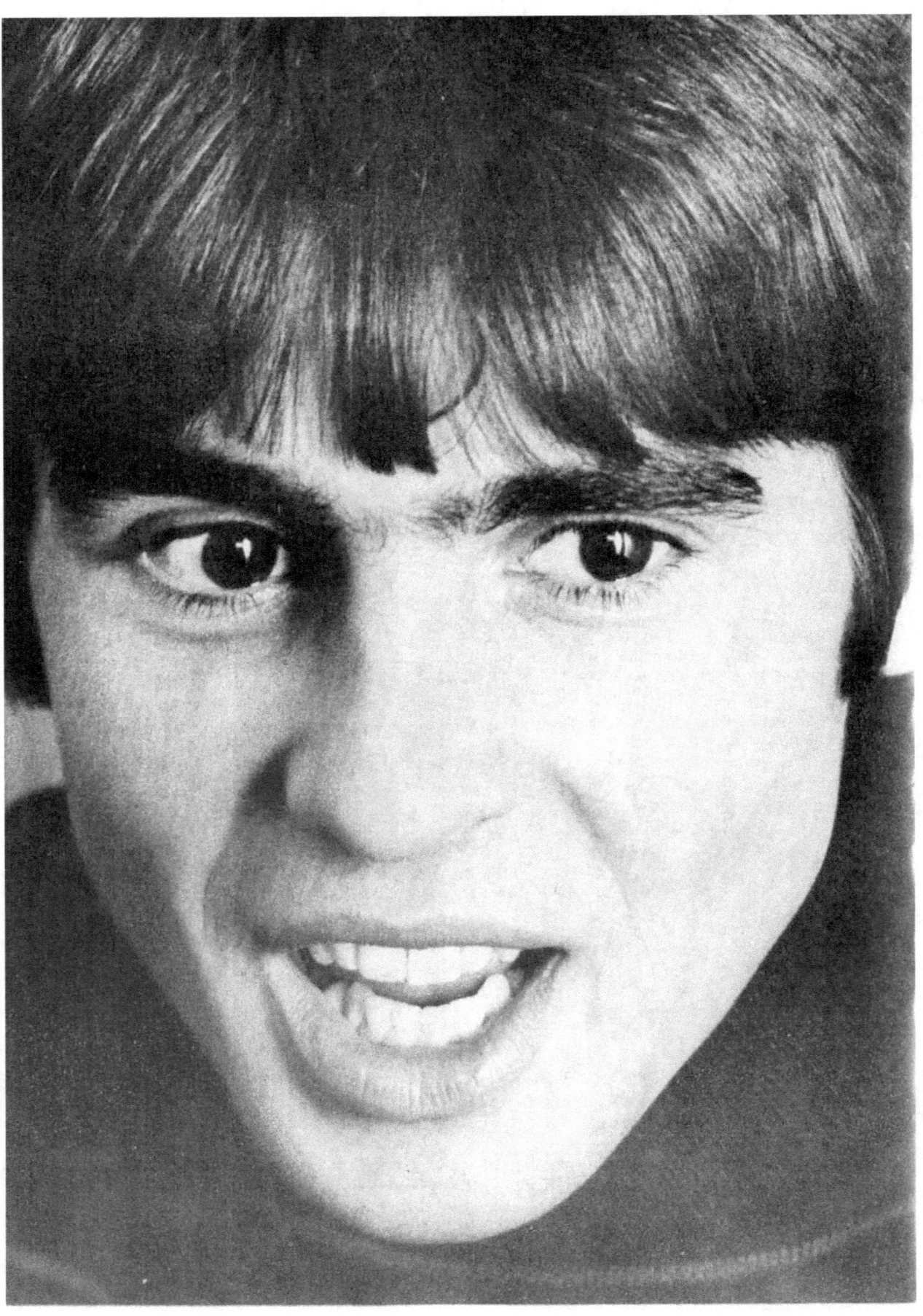

DAVY

YOU SHOULD HAVE TOLD US!

Special Report by Jackie Richmond

OH, Davy, you should have told us! Davy, love, why did you have to leave us to find out about your marriage and your baby in the most soul-shocking way of all . . . through blown-up headlines in the national newspapers? Why didn't you let us, your fans, into the secret?

Since the news broke that you married Linda some 18 months ago, our phones have never stopped ringing. So many stories about the Monkees have appeared in the national press and so many have been downright untrue, that lots of your most loyal fans felt there was just a chance that this story, too, was inaccurate.

MARRIED

But, of course, it wasn't. You are married and you are a dad and a lot of fans still feel numb about the way they heard the news. So now all the Monkees are married. But, that's not half the tragedy that some of the Fleet Street newsmen have made it. That's not why I ask again; Oh, Davy, why did you do it?

Remember your last visit to Britain? You sat, legs swinging, in your publicist's office chatting away merrily to all of us? Remember being asked pointblank; "Any plans for marriage . . .?" Remember, most important, saying, and I quote; "There are so many beautiful girls in the world and I've only seen some of them. There's plenty of time for marriage but, right now, it's just not my scene"?

You were actually married at that time, Davy.

Remember telling me on the phone from America; "I would have proposed, maybe, to Lulu—she's a great girl. But I feel marriage at this stage would tie me down. There's so much for me yet to do in my career."

You were actually married at that time.

Now you have said, and I respect your feelings, that you feel you give a lot of yourself through your career. That you have the glare of publicity upon you most of the time and that you simply have to keep your personal life to yourself. That is fair enough. We, the fans, appreciate that you must be able to lead your own life with the prying eyes of cameras and the loaded questions of reporters.

ADVISERS

But why DO pop stars sometimes feel that if they get married it has to be kept completely quiet? One theory is that they, or their advisers, feel that the fans would depart. The star is no longer "available". Perhaps there was some truth in that in the early days of the pop boom. Even so, John Lennon didn't

MONKEES ARCHIVES 3

STOP PRESS...STOP PRESS...STOP

"Mirror" breaks the news

The news that Davy was married some time ago and already has a little daughter was broken by Don Short in the *Daily Mirror* on June 7. It caused a big stir in the pop world.

One important fact was missed by most journalists and that is how on earth did Davy manage to keep it a secret for so long.

Many people must have been "in the know" but everyone kept the secret. He can certainly trust his friends!

PROUD FATHERS

All of the Monkees are proud fathers. Each one is also certain that his daughter is the prettiest girl in the state.

They have certainly chosen original names for their beautiful babies. We have already told you how Micky came to choose Ami Bluebell, and now, of course, Davy has revealed that Thalia is of Greek origin.

GOOD REACTIONS TO NEW RELEASES

Both the Monkees' new single "Listen To The Band" and their LP "Instant Replay" have been greeted with considerable enthusiasm by the music paper reviewers. Especially some who previously have been rather critical of recent singles released by the boys.

At present, "Listen To The Band" is steadily climbing in the American Top 100 but it has got quite a way to go to reach the Top 10.

In this country, many regard their new single as being a forerunner to a new type of disc which will be released by the Monkees trio in future.

SEPTEMBER TOUR?

Vic Lewis of Nems Enterprises is still hoping to bring the boys over to this country in September. He told the "MONKEES MONTHLY" "All the boys are very anxious to return to this country and they particularly want to perform in the cities outside London as their only previous personal appearances were at Wembley."

MICKY'S HOUSE

"MONKEES MONTHLY" readers have seen several pictures of Micky's Laurel Canyon home.

What hasn't been revealed before is that his house is the oldest building in this exclusive area of California and was actually the first to be put up by hunters at the turn of the century.

Micky and Samantha have made many changes, but they have done their best to preserve the original parts of the building because of their historic associations with the past.

NO CLUBBING NOW

All the Monkees were enthusiastic club-goers during 1967 and 1968. But, nowadays, all the boys spend most evenings at home with their friends.

In fact, their wives report that they even help with the preparation of meals and washing-up afterwards.

MONKEES ARCHIVES 3

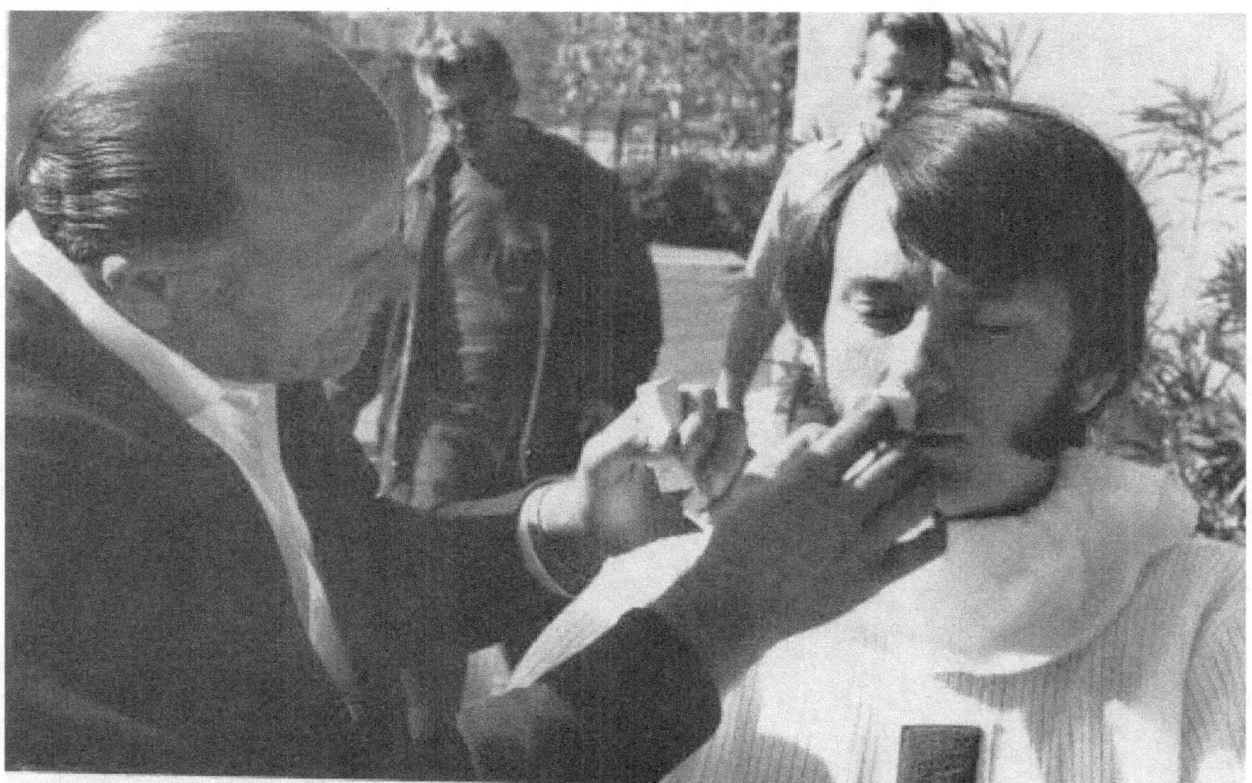

ABOVE: The make-up man gets busy on Mike for the scenes at Pasadena.

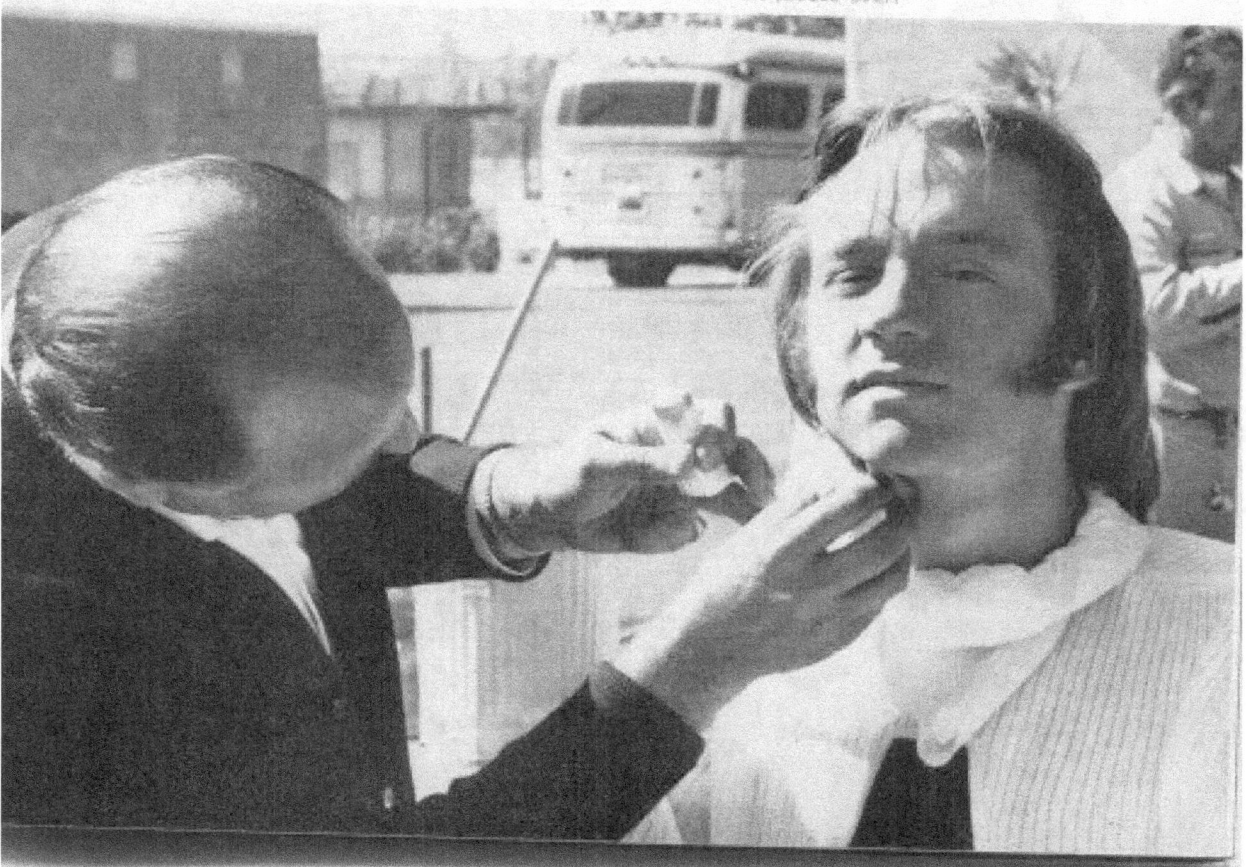

BELOW: Now it's Peter's turn to sit still and be fussed over.

MONKEES ARCHIVES 3

ABOVE: Davy makes with the hands while Peter does his take-off of a London Bobbie
BELOW: Mike chats to one of the film crew.

WAR!

By Our Stateside Reporter

As I told you last month, Davy, Micky, Mike and Peter plus the film crew made a special trip to the Rose Bowl, Pasadena to film sequences for their first major movie.

Special costumes had been designed for the sequence. All the boys wore white slippers, white trousers and polo-necked jumpers. The first person I saw walking round the Bowl was Peter with a large 'A' on his chest. Then Mike turned up with a large exclamation mark. Even when Dave and Micky arrived with a 'W' and 'R' respectively emblazoned on their jumpers, I still didn't get it. Then, they all filed on to the green turf of the Football pitch and lined up and there it was—a big W.A.R.!

Davy, on the left, looks as though he is bowling one of the fastest balls delivered at Lords cricket ground—in actual fact, he just leaped into the air shaking his fist; over the page you can see that Peter is producing the most frantic leap of all.

None of the Monkees realised that the film might be given an 'X' Certificate in England until I pointed it out to them and I can tell you that when Davy realised what I was getting at, he said: "We'll make sure that it doesn't happen." So, it looks as though every Monkee fan will be able to see every second of the picture when it's finally released in this country.

MONKEES ARCHIVES 3

MONKEES ARCHIVES 3

MONKEES ARCHIVES 3

PETER TORK'S LIFE IN PIX
By Mrs. CATHERINE McGUIRE STRAUS

Peter's "Grams" invites you to peek over her shoulder while she turns the pages of the Thorkelson family photo album back to the years before Peter became a world-famous Monkee!

Can you find Peter in this Carleton College class photo? He's near the upper right, in striped jacket and narrow tie. The girl with glasses sitting beside him was his "big romance". She's married now—but they are still friends.

MONKEES ARCHIVES 3

Take a look at the lovely "Thorkelson kids". Left to right, they are Christopher, Peter, Anne and Nicky. This picture was taken at the family home in Connecticut when Peter was 15 years old.

Who's this lovely lady? It's Peter's mom Ginny. This is her favorite picture of herself.

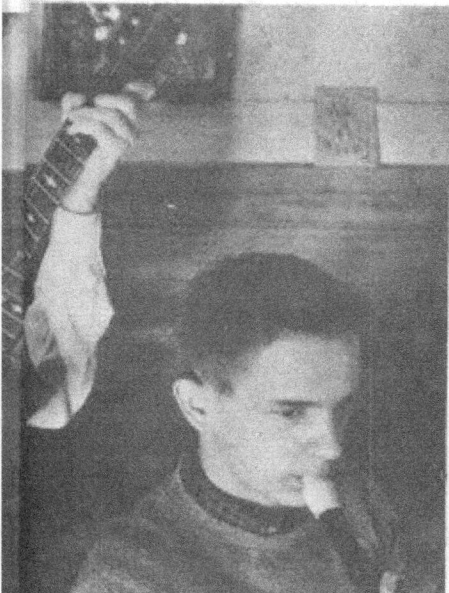
Peter plays guitar and Nicky plays recorder at one of their "jam sessions". Peter was home for a weekend. He was 20 years old and had just moved to Greenwich Village in New York City.

We all went to Brazil for Christmas in 1963. Peter is at the top left, and I am seated at right.

Back in Connecticut, Nicky and Peter pose in the library for a family photo.

Here's an adorable picture Peter snapped of Chris and Anne when he was home for Christmas in 1965.

This handsome lad is also Chris. This picture was taken when the family went on a tour of England in the spring of 1966.

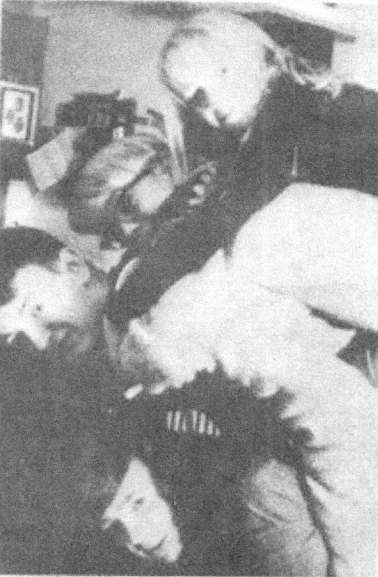
The "Thorkelson kids" gang up on each other! That's Peter on the bottom. Then come Nicky, Chris and Anne. This was taken in Regina, Canada, in the winter of 1966.

MONKEES ARCHIVES 3

RASCALS RAID THE MONKEES SHOW!

The very first visitors invited by the Monkees themselves to do a guest interview on their TV show were Gene Cornish and Dino Danelli of the Rascals. (Unfortunately, Eddie and Felix were not available, as they were over-dubbing some of the bands on the Rascals' new LP).

Slowly, slowly, they ——— trip along from pix to pix and see for yourself!

What have we here? A magic piece of paper? Watch out Davy, it might explode!

Whoosh—abracadabra! Our genies are about to reveal their great secret—!

Why, I do believe it's the album cover for the Rascals' new Atlantic LP, Once Upon A Dream!

MONKEES ARCHIVES 3

Gene explains that the back cover symbolically represents the Rascals' "future".

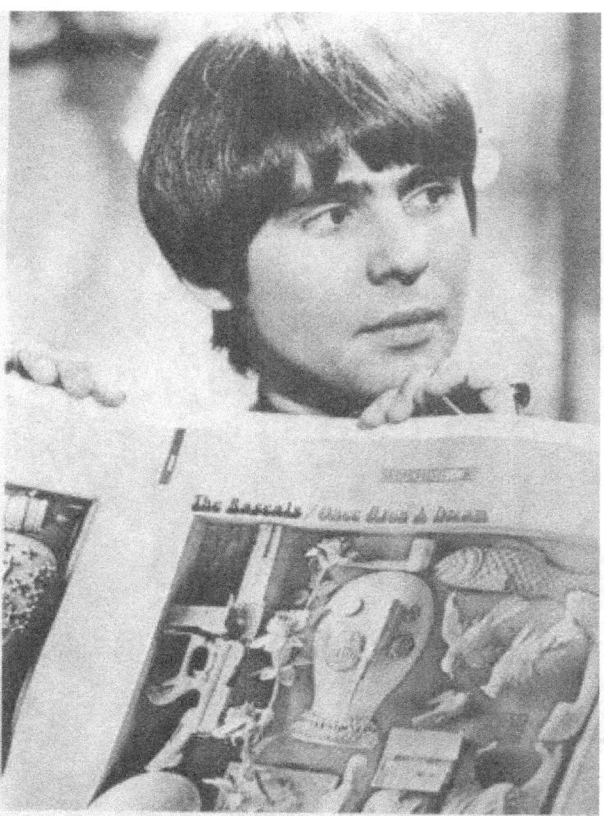
Davy listens while Dino explains that the front cover represents the Rascals "today".

Dino, who designed the cover, looks pleased about the whole thing.

Stay tuned to the Monkees show, so you won't miss this fabulous trio!

MONKEES ARCHIVES 3

MONKEES REVEAL... "the t

DAVY JONES

I HATE to be kept waiting. In fact, if anyone ever leaves me waiting—well, when they get to where I'm *supposed* to be, I'm usually gone!

I HATE to be linked romantically with girls I hardly know or with girls who are just friends. *It happens all the time and confuses everyone.*

I HATE people who make fun of other people's shortcomings. There is something wrong with each and every one of us, and we should think of that before we poke fun at others.

I HATE to have our soft-ball game stopped. A bunch of us play ball every weekend, and it really bugs me when somebody stops us right in the middle of an exciting moment to ask me to pose for a picture or to write an autograph. They should wait 'til the end of the inning, and then I wouldn't mind doing anything at all.

I HATE fans who say that they're sick or seriously ill in order to get a phone call from me. I care deeply not only for my fans but for my fellow human beings, and if I think a little girl is in real need and I can help—I'll do everything I can. But lately there have been some unprincipled kids who have deliberately "made up" stories about being on their death-beds, etc., to get a call from me. And when I call and find out that they just did it to get to me, it really hurts me. I mean—what is the world coming to when somebody can pull a terrible trick like that? It makes me lose faith in people.

I HATE to see girls have an inferiority complex because they're too short or too tall, or something like that. My heart really goes out to them. A good rule for us all to practice is to remember that "there is something good in everybody, seek it, then make it grow". In other words, forget about the negatives and think about the positives—and everything will be all right!

I HATE to see parents put their kids down because they have long hair, dig rock and roll, or belong to the "now" generation. I say that each generation has its own moment and it's the *groovy* "folks" who let their kids live their moment to the fullest.

I HATE disrespectful young people. When I see a kid be rude to an adult (and especially to a much older person) it really makes my blood boil. Right or wrong, we all owe respect to our elders.

I HATE people who exploit the Monkees for money or publicity. For instance, a security guard in one town recently said that we "beat" him up and he sued us for a whole lot of money. What really happened was that Micky was trying to rush into a hotel and the guard didn't recognize him and refused to let him in. Micky had a choice between being torn apart by overly-enthusiastic fans or pushing his way into the lobby of the hotel. He did the latter. Believe me, that's all that happened—nobody "beat" anybody up!

I HATE for a girl to "yes" me because she thinks it will make me like her more.

I LOVE animals, but I guess that's no secret since I have three cats, two dogs, two rabbits and an aquarium—well, practically a zoo at my house!

I LOVE my new haircut. It's a little shorter and it comes down pointed in front of my ears, like sideburns.

I LOVE to get a suntan and I really think I'm happiest when I'm lying around by my swimming pool, soaking up the sun.

I LOVE birds and I have built an aviary (that's a kind of big communal outdoor nest) in my backyard. All the friendly neighborhood birds fly there to nest, rest, eat or just goof around.

I LOVE farm animals, and by the time you read this I will probably have gotten myself two sheep!

I LOVE girls who are feminine, but who have an independent streak in them.

I LOVE horses, and recently Basil Foster, an old friend of mine from Manchester, and I bought two yearlings at Middleham. The horses are named Chico-mono (Spanish for "little monkey") and Pearl Locker, and they are kept at the Newmarket stables, where I used to be an apprentice jockey. (Don't tell anybody, but every weekend I phone Middleham to see how they are!)

I LOVE my "fans," whom I prefer to call friends. I had so very much hoped that we Monkees would go on the road this summer, so that I could meet some more of you super 16-ers. Well, maybe soon. Meanwhile, there is still our movie to look forward to.

I LOVE our movie. We finally found a name for it. We're just gonna call it *Head*. That's it, man—just plain *Head*.

I LOVE clothes so much that I not only have a clothing store on the East Coast, but I'm thinking of opening another clothing store here in Hollywood. There's a building at Santa Monica and Crescent in which I will probably locate the store, and if I do decide to go ahead with it I hope that Gene Ashman (who designed most of our Monkee gear) will design a special Davy Jones line of clothes just for my store.

I LOVE warm, friendly, sparkly girls.

I LOVE to eat fresh fruits and vegetables.

I LOVE to read letters from you—and if you have time, I'd like for you to drop me a line at Box 1498, Beverly Hills, California.

ings we HATE & the things we LOVE!"

PETER TORK

I HATE *hate*. I mean, in the sense that some people mean it. The way I am using it here is just as a strong word to indicate the things that displease me, put me down, drag me and turn me off.

I HATE dependent people. I mean, someone who has no will, drive or goals of their own. People who need others to "support" them, their moods, their very existence.

I HATE girls who come on tough, aggressive, and in a show-offy manner.

I HATE girls who don't like being girls. You know, the kind who wear slacks all the time and don't comb their hair or take care of their nails—and like that.

I HATE stupidity. I guess there are some people who can't help being a little backward, but most people just don't stay awake! It really turns me off to see people sleep their way through this beautiful life.

I HATE repetitive people. I've got good ears and a fairly good mind, and it drags me when someone tells me the same thing twice or several times.

I HATE sloppiness — like people who come to your house and drop things all about and don't clean up after themselves.

I HATE pushy people, especially those who sort of move in and don't know when it's time to quit, split and go home.

I HATE prejudice and violence. Somehow, those two seem to go hand-in-hand. Think of it this way: suppose we lived in a country where everybody was green, and then some orange and purple polka-dotted people came along. Soon we would be saying, "Gee, what funny-looking polka-dotted people!" But because people are basically good in their hearts, each group would want to be friendly with the other. It's only fear, lies and bad leadership that keeps us all from loving each other and from seeing each other clearly and purely with the eye of the mind and the love of the heart.

I LOVE music in all forms. I especially love to compose. I have written many songs and — who knows? — maybe one day I will make a recording of them just for you.

I LOVE comfortable clothes made of soft fabrics and I have a weakness for handmade American Indian moccasins.

I LOVE conversations full of quick, witty remarks. There is nothing more stimulating to me than engaging in a debate with a well-informed, articulate person.

I LOVE people and I have a particular fondness for children and animals. I have quite a collection of pussycats and puppy dogs (most of them given to me by fans), and they have free run of my new house in an isolated area in Studio City.

I LOVE sauna baths — that's a kind of "dry heat" room made of pine wood. It's very relaxing to sit in one for awhile and then to dive into a cold swimming pool. Wow!

I LOVE my fans. By that, I mean all of you young people out there who, with your fantastic energy and devotion, elevated us Monkees from relative obscurity to a position where we're able to communicate with millions of people—not just to give our music and our acting talent, but to give our innermost thoughts. I hope that somehow I have been able to repay you for all that you have done for me.

I LOVE reading anything I can lay my hands on, but I'm particularly into far eastern philosophy. For instance, did you know that according to an ancient Upanishad ". . . on the tree of life within us sits two birds. One eats, pecks, scratches and gets on with living in general. The other watches, always silent, always awake, always fully aware—unless you let him fall asleep." If he falls asleep, the other bird goes on pecking and scratching away without any *meaning* to his life. If *you* keep the second bird awake, he guides the first bird to higher and higher levels, so that one day they both become one being—full of bliss, consciousness and wisdom.

Don't miss the next issue of 16 Magazine, cos next month Micky Dolenz and Mike Nesmith reveal the things they hate and the things they love! The January issue of 16 goes on sale November 26! Watch for it!

MONKEES ARCHIVES 3

"COME TO THE MONKEES' FIRST BIG PARTY!"
BY JEFF NEAL

You are Jeff's date as he escorts you to the Main Ballroom of The Barbizon Plaza Hotel in New York City where you meet—

THE MONKEES!—long before they become famous!

IN SEPTEMBER of 1966—just over a year ago—none of us could guess how big the Monkees were going to be. I (because I was fortunate enough to be a long-time good friend of David Jones) got the following invitation in the morning mail:

> Michael Dolenz, Michael Nesmith, Peter Tork and David Thomas Jones invite you to a party in the Main Ballroom of The Barbizon Plaza Hotel in New York City at 6:30 P.M. on September 12, 1966.

"MYSTERY" PARTY

Since Davy was a special friend of mine, I was very thrilled. I got dressed in my "finest"—a dark suit, white shirt and tie—and at 6:30 P.M. on the nose I arrived at the appointed place. Use your imagination now, pretend that you are my date, and come along with me to the Monkees' "mystery" party!

A straight-faced young man wearing a green wool hat greets us at the door. I know who he is because Davy has told me all about the Monkees.

"I'm Michael Nesmith," he says, and we shake hands.

Mike escorts us inside and the first person to greet us is dynamic David Jones. After I introduce you, Davy takes your arm and escorts us around. The first two people we meet are David's Hollywood buddy, David Pearl and Monkees' producer Bert Schneider. After exchanging greetings, we turn and find ourselves staring into the faces of Micky Dolenz and Peter Tork. I had spoken to Micky on the phone a couple of times, because he and Davy were sharing a house in Hollywood.

"So you're the guy who wakes me up in the morning!" Micky exclaims, and pretends he is about to strangle me.

"Hold on there, son," Peter says, feigning shock." Don't harm a hair on this young man's head!"

In no time we find ourselves chitchatting with these two super-nice Monkees, and we both are delighted that they are so unbelievably kind. Suddenly, the lights start flashing on and off in the ballroom and everyone is asked to sit down. We find ourselves seated together, surrounded by Monkees and staring up at a large screen. The lights go out and the very first Monkees segment begins to unreel—in living color—before our very eyes! Everyone who saw that show was

CONTINUED ON PAGE 30

A straight-faced young man . . .

MONKEES ARCHIVES 3

"COME TO THE MONKEES' FIRST BIG PARTY!"

CONTINUED FROM PAGE 20

thrilled—so you can understand that the thrill was even *greater for us,* sitting there and seeing it with the boys for the very first time. After laughing our way through the pilot film—before we know it—it is over. There is a split second of silence, then the room is filled with thunderous applause. Everyone hurries around, telling everyone else how great, great, *great,* GREAT the Monkees are! Mike, David, Micky and Peter are grinning with delight, but saying nothing.

MONKEE FEEDING TIME!

Micky runs over and throws open the double doors at one side of the room—and stretched out before us is a tremendous banquet table loaded with everything from appetizers to roast beef to jello! "Feeding time at the zoo" turns out to be almost as fantastic a success as the show has been. There are six different salads, eight different main dishes, four ice cream desserts, three different jellos and all the cake and pastries you can eat (if you have any room left in your tummy, that is!)

After we (along with Mike) find a table and sit down with our heavily-laden trays, Davy comes over and joins us. The first thing he asks us it, "Tell the *truth.* Did you like the show?"

There is a verbal stampede for a moment as we both compete trying to tell the guys how outasite we both know the Monkees series *shall* and *will* be. Finally, we convince the guys and they relax, and we all enjoy a quiet dinner punctuated by humor and a feeling of "togetherness" that you and I will never forget . . .

As I said before, it is over a year since that special and very wonderful night. But if you are anything like me, you not only dug every show last season *and* the re-runs all summer *and* this season's even greater Monkees show—but you also have become a loving and loyal Monkees fan forever!

Co-hosts—in the Beginning.

MONKEES ARCHIVES 3

The Truth About

NOW IT CAN BE TOLD!

Peter's Marriage

By Ann Moses

It all began with a letter from a Monkee fan, and in particular a Peter fan. I received her letter in the Tiger Talk mail and decided to print it since I thought her ideas were unusual and needed to be shared. I couldn't understand what "kind of person" Peter had been branded by the girl, but here at Tiger Beat we feel *every* opinion is important. Her letter read:

EX-PETER FAN
Peter Tork has always been my fave Monkee until I found out he had been married and divorced! I was furious! I never thought Peter was that kind of person! So now Davy's my fave Monkee.

Brenda Rednour
Pascagoula, Miss.

It was only a matter of weeks before letters began to flood my office from fans in defense of Peter. Every single letter was outraged at Brenda's thoughts and put her down for her narrow-mindedness. I thought it was fantastic that Peter's fans were so loyal, but more than that—they had obviously picked up on his belief that you should judge every person on his own merit, not by his color, his creed *or his past!* I wonder if Brenda ever thought that Peter is what he is today because of *all* the experiences he's had throughout his life.

When I brought all the letters to Peter, he felt it was necessary to make an explanation to his fans. Here, in his own words, is what he told me:

MONKEES ARCHIVES 3

The first time I laid eyes on Jody she was standing at the head of the stairs at the Four Winds Cafe on West Third Street in Greenwich Village. She had her feet about three feet apart, her arms folded, and she was glaring defiantly on the street filled with long-haired weirdos and the even weirder tourists. She looked at me and said, "Ya got a cigarette?"

I had been working at the Four Winds regularly, but I'd taken a couple of days off and during that time she had come to work as a waitress. We hit it off right away. She really was brassy, full of her own spunk and fire. I really flipped out. I really liked that in her. I love that brassy, "get out of my way, Charlie, if you don't have anything to do with what I'm doing" way. She was totally self-contained.

LOVE AT FIRST SIGHT

It was really love at first sight. I found out that she was the child of a couple divorced very early in life, raised only by her mother, and she had been alone a lot. She was very interested in horses. I find that people that are terribly hung up in horses, the way Jody was anyway, are using it because their experiences in the people world have left them very disillusioned. Jody thought so too, that's why she came to the Village, specifically to try and get back into people.

We started going together and we were really, really hitting it off. We were a team socking it to everybody; and doing good works. She was 16 and I was 22. I can remember I was walking around with this constant grin on my face. I just couldn't stop smiling!

HAD TO BE TOGETHER

We finally felt pressured into marriage. She was under age, legally speaking, although not to me, but we felt we had to get married to try and maintain any kind of unity together. We were young and we felt we had to be together. We were certainly enough in love. We said, "no doubt in our minds." We were just heavy into each other and ready. The problem was we had no idea what kind of emotional readjustment marriage takes.

It's like marrying is getting back your parent of the opposite sex. A woman marries a man because of her father and a man marries a woman because of his mother. You're both searching for your parent in the form of someone your own age.

JODY WAS YOUNG

Now Jody, at 16, was hardly my contemporary much less a mother. She was all willing to cuddle and hold, but I think she was cuddling her father and not her husband. A wife has to be both a mother and a wife to a man and the man has to be both a father and a husband. It all has to mix in and tie up.

So why couldn't we make it work? Life is what you make it. When we first got married we said we were going to stick together for two years whether we were together or not, as a married thing. But after a month and half we separated and moved into our own places and after 18 months we got a divorce.

THE BIG ADJUSTMENT

There were so many things that contributed to our breaking up I couldn't recount them all. I think most of the problems centered around not being emotionally ready for the great readjustment marriage requires.

For example, Jody didn't feel capable of giving time to being both my social partner—like going out everywhere—and still doing the dishes at home. Like they're be dishes when company came and I'd pick on her for it, I mean, really make an issue because I didn't know any better. I was a blind, fool kid.

WHEN SHE LEFT

After a while she said, "I'm not going to take this abuse," and went to leave. I said, "You're not going to leave!" She said, "I am too!" And it was beat, bash, belt— I mean I actually hit her once. And that was it. She split.

MONKEES ARCHIVES 3

After we were separated she took a separate place and I would drop by every so often. Once in a while it would be pretty comfortable. There was always enough tension to keep us from flinging into each other's arms, but it was comfortable enough to where we could discuss it a little bit and skirt the edges of the issue. After the divorce she went to Paris and got into horses again.

SEEING JODY NOW

I've since seen Jody a number of times. She came back to New York for a while after Paris and she now lives in San Francisco. On her way to San Francisco she stopped here in Los Angeles to see what it was all about. When we're comfortable together now, the spark is back. And it's stunning again, it dazzles me! But when it's not there it just puts me up so tight I don't want to see her. If Jody was to come back suddenly and everything clicked and everything was cool, it would be new. It would be like it was some other girl, because we've both changed so much.

Jody's reaction to the whole Monkee thing is she regards it only as public recognition of what she's already known, as I do. She's really capable of great business ability. If she took over an office, she'd make it a success. She already has. There's a thing called Personality Posters for which she opened international offices.

REACTION TO FANS

About the girl who wrote in to Tiger Talk and said she was no longer a fan of mine, all I can say is she's welcome to her opinion. Right and wrong are her business only. If I'm doing, or did, something that for her is wrong, if it's impossible for her to like me any further, I say carry on. God bless you, say I.

I don't think I'll ever get married again. I used to say way back before that I didn't think I'd ever get married, but then I did. I still say I'll never get married again, but I probably will. I'll get married when it's demanded by society, if I choose to run for office. Then I'd probably marry whoever I was going with at the time to have a wife.

WORTHWHILE EXPERIENCE

The entire experience had a great effect on me. I remember three weeks after my marriage broke up I was sitting there shattered, wondering what had happened to me. How could I have lost myself?

I was pacifist at the time and here I was hitting a poor little girl, much younger and much smaller than me—really hitting her! Where was that at? It really brought me face to face with a lot of convictions that I'd held sort of on the surface and I hadn't had a real confrontation with. Friends of mine remarked as little as three weeks after Jody had left that the whole experience had cleared my head out and it made a man out of me, right there and then.

The experience took me to the very bottom of my life. I needed it. Experiences like this, if they don't break you, they strengthen you. I don't believe much in people saying "it was a miserable time in my life, I wish I'd never gone through it." If such an experience leaves you shakey and neurotic for the rest of your life, then maybe it's an experience you could have done without. But most everyone who recovers from a really heavy experience is the stronger for it. I am, and I *know*.

MONKEES ARCHIVES 3

The Monkees in London

CHAPTER 2

by SAMANTHA JUSTE

"Sammy" tells it like it was when the Monkees hit England on their summer concert tour!

PROBABLY THE GREATEST THING to hit England since the "Beatle Invasion" of several years ago was the arrival of the Monkees for their series of London concerts this past summer. They were to perform in our Wembley Pool, which is one of our largest arenas—and all the tickets had been sold out for weeks and weeks in advance.

The Monkees' opening concert was on a Friday evening and they decided to spend that entire afternoon rehearsing. Getting Mike, Micky, Peter and Davy to and from Wembley was handled like a military operation. The boys arrived for rehearsal in a clapped-out old catering truck that looked like it was delivering bread and rolls more than anything else! A security guard sneaked them in right under the noses of thousands of fans who had crowded around hoping to see a real live Monkee off-stage. After a very long and tiring rehearsal, it came time to leave and a second security team went into action. They put four boys—who (from a distance) looked just like the Monkees—into a limousine with smoked dark windows and drove off. The limousine took a real beating, but the decoy worked and the Monkees themselves were spirited away right behind it in a less obvious car.

FANTASTIC OPENING NIGHT

The Monkees were rather nervous about their first London concert and each boy was secretly hoping for a good reception. Well, they needn't have worried. The greeting their English fans gave them surpassed their wildest dream! The Pool was packed and the audience was well behaved while Lulu and the other performers gave a very good show.

After intermission, Micky, Mike, Davy and Peter hopped upon the stage and it was like millions of sky rockets had been shot off! One was literally caught up into the vibrating sea of sound which greeted each move the Monkees made and each song they sang! There is no way to describe it. I only hope you are lucky enough—if you have not already had the experience—to get to see a real, *live* Monkee concert one day, then you will know what I mean.

SHOPPING ON KING'S ROAD

The following Saturday morning, Micky went to our newest mod shopping area, King's Road, to see what he could find. He stopped in Dandy Fashions, one of London's newest boutiques, where he bought a long Edwardian jacket in shiny white brocade, an orange silk shirt and red boots!

Of course, he was spotted right off and I witnessed what can only be called "the magical Dolenz touch"—when it comes to handling excited crowds. Micky stood in the doorway and held up his hand until everyone was quiet. Then he spoke to them.

"If you don't mind sort of lining up," he said gently, "I will be glad to sign all the autographs you want. But please don't push and shove me."

The Monkees were a smash in their London concerts. Here, Davy

Micky blasts the drums—

MONKEES ARCHIVES 3

The Monkees at their London press conference.

The fans calmed down and happily did exactly what Micky had asked—and every last one of them got a personal Micky Dolenz autograph without any trouble at all before he left!

The next two concerts were also smashes, and everyone was rather amazed that there weren't any catastrophes among the more than 50,000 people who came to see the Monkees. One 14-year-old girl fell off the balcony where she had been jumping up and down with great enthusiasm. She wasn't seriously hurt, but the Monkees didn't want to leave the hall after the show until each of them had been personally assured that she was all right. One lucky girl got to do what every Monkee fan dreams of doing—during the show she somehow broke through the cordon of police and jumped onto the stage. She was hugging Micky (who hugged her back, but kept right on singing) before the guards literally unwrapped her arms from him and took her away!

MONKEE PARTY-TIME

Vic Lewis, of Nems Enterprises (the organization in charge of the series of Monkee concerts), threw a tremendous party for the Monkees at London's swinging Speakeasy Club after their last concert. Davy who had gone off to see his father, was not there—but everyone else was. John Lennon arrived with his wife Cynthia, and George and Pattie Harrison came with Paul McCartney and Jane Asher. Eric Clapton of the Cream was there, as were Keith Moon of the Who, Manfred Mann and Mike d'Abo (of the Mann group), Lulu and swarms of other pop people. The rave-up didn't end until long after midnight!

When the Monkees arrived back at the Royal Garden Hotel, where they were staying, Micky saw a crowd of patient fans still waiting around outside. He stopped and talked to them for a while, then he led them into Hyde Park (which is right next door)—sort of like the Pied Piper. He got up on an old-fashioned bandstand and gave a non-stop performance of singing, joking, talking and clowning around for over an hour! Most of those fans were in tears by the time the police eventually broke up the "Dolenz concert." They were completely swept away, because a famous star had gone to all that trouble and effort just for them.

The next day the Monkees and most of their guests from the night before went to shop some more on King's Road. This time, they went to the Antique Supermarket, where the boys bought everything from beads to bells to Chinese robes!

TIME TO GO

All of a sudden it was time for the Monkees to leave England, and some of us went back to Heathrow Airport to see them off. As I waved goodbye, I mentally jotted down my very clear impression of each of the boys.

Peter is quiet and very calm. He seems vague at times, but he has definite opinions and expresses them. He is very much a musician and everywhere he goes, the guitar goes too.

Davy is very conscientious and works tremendously hard. At the same time, he seems very warm and cuddly—and the girls go wildest over him.

Mike is very serious and much quieter—but when he does say something, it is pretty much to the point and can often be devastating. He hides his fantastic sense of humor behind his reserve.

Micky is the livewire of the group. He has got more energy than one dozen people and he literally never seems to stop.

As a group, the Monkees are unique. I have never known a group who think so much of and care so much about one another. At the same time, they are completely frank and honest among themselves and never hesitate to speak their minds if they think one or another is goofing around too much.

By the time you read this, Peter, Mike, Micky and Davy will have finished their summer tour of the States and will be back working on future records and TV episodes. I only hope that somehow I can be around to continue to see them and perhaps be lucky enough to write more about them for you in *16* Magazine.

Mike puts the crowd in a frenzy —

—and Peter thumps away delightedly on his guitar.

MONKEES ARCHIVES 3

Hermits. We stopped at all the "In" places. Phyllis and I especially liked the Cromwell Inn. . . . And then we went out to stay with the Lennons, and that really was an unbelievably wonderful experience. . . .

"John and I established a great rapport. We were like kindred spirits. Believe me, it was really a great meeting of the minds—although I guess some people might think of a Beatle and a Monkee meeting as a crazy or funny event.

"Actually, John and I are just two guys who are doing what makes us happy, and being around each other was terribly stimulating. . . . He has a fabulous mind. I listened to him a great deal, and when I talked, he was not unimpressed. . . .

"It really was a marvelous experience for both Phyllis and I. She and Cynthia had as much rapport as John and I did. Frankly, right now John and Cynthia Lennon are about the only other couple in the world who Phyllis and I can be with and share the same experiences. . . .

"Also, it was very interesting to compare notes with John on a strictly professional level. Because I have written some of the Monkees' songs, and of course John and Paul McCartney have composed most of the Beatles' biggest hits, we launched into a marvelous conversation about composing, record sessions, and such things.

"John's also got a lot of great tape recording equipment at home that we fooled around with. I had a ball trying to learn how to play his Meletron. It's such a complex thing that it would take about a week to explain it. It's a keyboard instrument similar to a piano, but it makes all sorts of fantastic sounds that duplicate other instruments. . . ."

While Mike took a few breaths, Phyllis picked up the story.

"As wonderful as it all is, in a way it's sad for the boys. I mean, with both the Beatles and the Monkees, fame forces them to do one of two things—to perform, to face the public on stage, or to work in front of the cameras, and then to go home and hide behind their walls.

"The Beatles hide with their millions. In a way, they're really trapped. They just can't go anywhere. Why, do you know what John Lennon said to Mike? He said, 'Thank God for the Monkees, you've taken the heat off of us.'

"I must say Cynthia and I had a wonderful time being together while Mike and John were off talking. We cooked, and sat around, and traded stories about our babies. It really was such a calm, quiet, warm relationship that sprang up between us. They certainly are fine people. They made our stay in England so very memorable.

"Their home—I guess you'd call it very old English style—is big, several stories high. They have a lot of nice things, but the overall feeling is one of simple warmth and graciousness. It's done so tastefully—very subdued—the carpets and walls are dark and rich looking, and in a way quite traditional.

"Their living room reminded me of ours. I mean there were newspapers around. . . . Don't misunderstand, I don't mean it was messy. . . . It's just that their house looks lived in and very inviting. . . ."

Mike had caught his breath, and he wanted to add something at this point. "You know, it really is quite amazing how much the four of us are alike. We're all home-bodies. . . . Both John and I are devoted to our wives and feel the same way about our children. . . . Cynthia and Phyllis are both so warm and wonderful and down-to-earth. . . . Well, I know it sounds repetitious, but really I think we could have traveled the whole world and never have found two people so close to us—people who thought as we did, and lived as we did, who experienced what we did, and who felt as grateful as we did for all that's happened.

"You know, when I was with John, he represented to me the pinnacle of the kind of success that The Monkees are now beginning to enjoy. . . . When I saw how he was able to accept everything, and to remain so enthusiastic and productive, it really drew us closer together. They say that music is an international language. Well, I think the rapport between *musicians*, such as John and myself, is also something which knows no barriers. . . . John may have an English accent, and I may speak *(Continued on page 55)*

PETER TORK'S SECRET PAST

CHAPTER 1
BY LANCE WAKELY

"The first time I saw Peter I didn't particularly notice his act, but when I heard his 'spiel' afterwards I nearly fell over."

THE FIRST TIME I saw Peter Tork was in a Greenwich Village "basket house" called The Pad. In those days, "basket houses" were all the rage. Unemployed singers and musicians would wander into a coffee house and, with the permission of the manager, would sing a few numbers and then hopefully pass a basket — explaining to the audience that *that* was the way they got paid. There were lots of guys who did this, but Peter was one of the most successful — and I might add that he never passed a basket; he passed his banjo. But we'll get to that later in the story.

In March, 1963, I arrived in the Village from Chicago. I had been playing acoustical guitar and had been singing for two years with groups and also alone. I had my own rock 'n' roll band in high school, and as a counsellor in summer camp I'd learned a lot about folk music. When I heard the Kingston Trio for the first time — that did it! I decided that I had to be a folk musician. I was 17 and too young to play in Chicago clubs, so I decided to go to New York — to the "great Greenwich Village" — where I "wood shed", "pay my dues" (meaning learning and rehearsing), and then go on to become a famous folk musician. I hitchhiked to New York and arrived in the Village, but I wasn't alone for long. It's easy to make friends there, and there's always someone who will put you up for a night.

The first time I saw Peter was in The Pad, where he had come to do a guest set. I later learned that he had been hanging

MONKEES ARCHIVES 3

around MàcDougal Street (we called it "Funnyville") for quite a few weeks. About that time Casey Anderson, a folk singer, was holding informal song-swapping sessions at a coffee house that used to be called Abdo's — and Peter used to play there, where he had already gained a reputation as a pretty good banjo picker. Actually, he stood out from the crowd, because he seemed to have a more complete formal music background than the others. For instance, he played the first baroque arrangement of an Elizabethan folk song that I had ever heard — and if you listen to Donovan's latest LP, you'll see that that is exactly what he (Donovan) is doing now.

Anyway, Peter (or Tork, as most of us called him) came into The Pad to do a "guest set" — that meant he was working in another coffee house, but came over to fill in for someone who couldn't make it to The Pad. He had practically no hair (by today's standards, that is) and it was combed straight back. He wore a red-checked hunting jacket, a blue sweat-shirt, beat-up jeans, dirty sneakers, a bedroll on his back and his banjo — which always hung around his neck. I didn't particularly notice his act, but when I heard his "spiel" afterwards I nearly fell over. He really knew how to get the customers to shell out.

"Ladies and gentlemen," he would say, with a great flourish, "as you know, we poor folk singers don't get paid by the management — so we are forced to pass the basket and place ourselves at your generous mercy. If you like what I've done, please make a contribution. This will help keep me off the streets at night, get me a good spaghetti dinner once in a while, and enable me to buy stamps to write home to dear old mom. Now, I'm going to pass my banjo around and if you put in silver *it* will go 'clink-clink,' but — ah! — if you put in folding money, *I* will go 'swishhh!' Now, if I go 'swishhh,' everybody will know that you are not only a music lover, but a great philanthropist."

At this point, Peter jumped off the stage and began to pass his banjo around. I was amazed at the "clinks" and "swishhhs" he got from the audience. He was really different; he was funny. He had more personality than all the rest. I remember thinking even then that Peter wasn't just a musician. He was more of an all 'round entertainer.

A few days later I bumped into Tork again, and became aware of another of his outstanding characteristics. He was friendly. In fact, he was *the friendliest guy in Greenwich Village!* He came right up to me and started talking. Soon, we were having coffee together, and soon we were planning to do sets together. Before I go into that, however, I must tell you about one particularly funny night when I dropped into the Playhouse Cafe while Peter was working alone.

"And now, ladies and gentlemen," I heard him saying, "I'm going to sing you a couple of original tunes. You may not know it, but I have a little brother who is a great songwriter. As a matter of fact, he's working on a complete musical score for the theatre right now. His name is Nick Tork, and you'll be hearing a lot about him one day." Then he launched into one of the most ridiculous and funny tunes I have ever heard. All I can remember about it is its title — *Under The Undertaker Gah-Goo-Gah*. When the audience "revived", Peter launched into another of his brother's ditties — all about an alligator named Albert, who got flushed down the toilet! Well, some of the Village cats may have sneered at that, but the audience ate it up — and Peter got even *more* "clinks" and "swishhhs" in his banjo!

Another thing about Peter was his *willingness*. Although all

"Under The Undertaker, Gah-Goo-Gah. . . ." *

His fingers — always losing by a note or two. *

MONKEES ARCHIVES 3

of us wanted to work in the "basket houses", it was hard to get one person to go on stage and get the show started. Peter would always do this — and in a very cheerful manner. He was that *somebody* you could count on. He was very dedicated to his music and very ambitious, and even though he had a lot to learn vocally and musically there was an aura about him that made all of us feel that if anybody was ever going to make it big time from the Village, it would be Peter Tork.

Peter was also very much the "imp" of the Village. He was like a funny genie, with a lock of hair falling across his forehead and a big smile on his face (except when he would grimace, stick his tongue out and perform various rubber-face antics for the audience). He was very popular with the girls who would come to the Village with their parents on a Sunday afternoon, and — believe it or not — many of the parents were straight-out Tork fans! His songs were accompanied by a good deal of light, humorous patter. In fact, he talked a *lot*. He sometimes tried to intellectualize his tales and often became tongue-tied and confused in doing so — which only made the audience love him all the more. He always "wrapped up" his act with a classical piece, carefully plucked out on his funky banjo, *sans* vocal. It usually ended in a race — with Peter's fingers always losing by a few notes here and there. But with his performance he left a happy house — and, as a result, he was very much in demand.

Along about this time I had become friendly with Ned, one of the Phoenix Singers, and I would stay in Ned's apartment while he was on the road. Peter and I were playing sets together now and then, and when Ned asked me to join the back-up group of the Phoenix Singers, he told me they were also looking for someone to replace a fellow named Steve, who had been drafted into military service. Steve played both guitar and banjo and Peter was the only guy in the Village I knew of who could do that too, so I recommended him.

At this point, Peter was living in a three-room, cold water flat on Bedford Street. You'd have to see the place to believe it. It came complete with assorted bugs (you name 'em—his pad had 'em, from roaches on down). Since neither of us could afford a choice in the matter, I moved in with him and we set about decorating the place in "contemporary side-street" (that is, discarded furniture we found in the various Greenwich Village alleyways) and Salvation Army specials. Believe it or not, we didn't even have a shower—so we used to have to "borrow" the shower of the two girls who lived upstairs!

Here's as good a time as any to talk about girls. Next to his music, girls interested Peter Tork more than anything else in the whole wide world. He loved them *all*—and most of them loved him. Peter wasn't tall, dark or handsome, but he made up for his liabilities with his great warmth, enthusiasm and sense of humor. He was also basically a very kind and giving person. He just had a way of making people happy even when he was broke, freezing cold and there were no prospects for work in the future. That Pied Piper-ish quality Peter had attracted girls of all shapes and sizes. He had many brief romances and a couple of very serious ones, and even to today Peter is still good friends with almost every girl he knew, dated, or fell in love with during his Greenwich Village days.

More about all that later — like in the April issue of 16. It goes on sale February 21. So I'll see you then!

But Peter always had a "rubber face" for Bob's camera!*

Peter as he looks today.

MONKEES ARCHIVES 3

DAVY JONES invites YOU —
"COME HOME WITH ME!"

JUST BEFORE CHRISTMAS, Davy Jones managed to grab a few free days — so he hurriedly packed and caught a plane for London, England. At London, he changed planes and flew to Manchester to spend a few precious days with his family. Davy Jones and *16 Magazine* extend a cordial invitation to you to join him on his visit home and to share the warmth of a good old-fashioned family get-together.

First of all, meet my relatives — rather **most** of them. Left to right are Alex (who is married to Lynda), my nephew Mark, his mom Lynda, me, my sister Beryl, and my dad Harry Thomas.

Well, it looks like I'm not the world's greatest baby-sitter, but I tried. By the way, my sister Hazel was not at home when these pictures were taken.

Here I am with my Scottie dog, "Dodger". In case you didn't notice, that's a **Monkee** I'm giving him.

MONKEES ARCHIVES 3

Here's the family — with me leading the way, natch — teaching Beryl how to cook. And it's a good thing, too — cos she was getting married the next day!

Hey, you'd be laughing, too, if you knew what happened. That's the postman in the middle, delivering the morning mail to my dad — and a letter from me was right on top!

Here my dad is hanging up one of the Christmas presents I gave him. It is a very unusual black and white painting one of my California buddies, Neko, did of me.

Thanks for coming along with me. Let's take "Dodger" for a final walk before we catch the plane back to Los Angeles. Hope we get together again real soon.

MONKEES ARCHIVES 3

MONKEES ARCHIVES 3

MONKEES ARCHIVES 3

My Life Story in Pix
BY PETER TORK

Take my hand and fly with me back through the years when I was a sweet young thing with never a thought that one day I would be a mad, mad *Monkee!*

CHAPTER ONE FIRST in a series that you simply must save if you're going to have a complete Peter Tork scrapbook

In the beginning there was me (at eight months) and my lovely mom, Virginia — but everyone calls her "Ginny." I started walking at nine months, shortly after this picture was taken in Washington, D.C., where I was born.

Here's a portrait of four generations. My mom, Virginia Hope Straus Thorkelson, is holding me, my grandad, Joseph Straus, is on the left. On the right is my great grandmother, Clementine K. Straus.

MONKEES ARCHIVES 3

Here I am, at just over a year old, in New York's Central Park with my mom's mom, Mrs. Catherine Straus — whom I nicknamed "Grams".

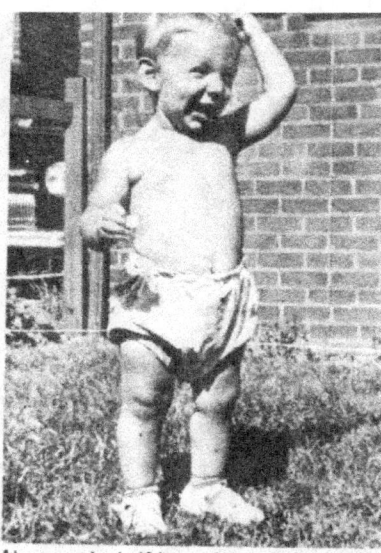
At one and a half in our backyard in Detroit — where my dad, John Holsten Thorkelson, took a job as an economist.

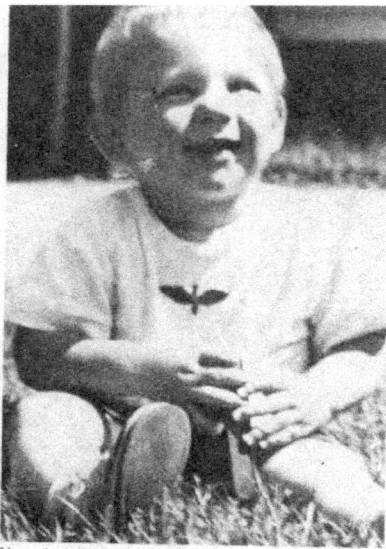
Now I am two years old and still in Detroit. My hair was pure white. In fact all the Thorkelsons had white hair during the early years of their lives

Meet the "tuffest" kid on the beach! "Grams" snapped this when I was three years old — when the family went to Long Island, N.Y., to spend the summer.

When I was three and a half, my father went into the service and was stationed in Berlin. That's me on the left, Nicky in the middle and dad on the right.

Meet "Addie," our Boxer dog. My family was still in Berlin, where we lived for one and a half years and where I learned to speak German fluently.

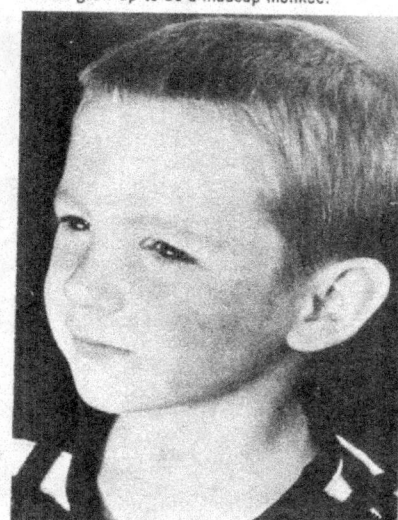
How do you like this portrait of me taken by my maid when I was five years old — still in Berlin? Who would have guessed that this sweet kid would grow up to be a madcap Monkee!

Whoops — our trip has been unexpectedly interrupted by lack of space. Never fear. I'll be right back here next month with the story of my life in exclusive pix. That'll be in the June issue of **16**, which will be on sale April 20. See ya' then. Meanwhile, turn the page for a super Peter Tork-type surprise.

THATAWAY

MONKEES ARCHIVES 3

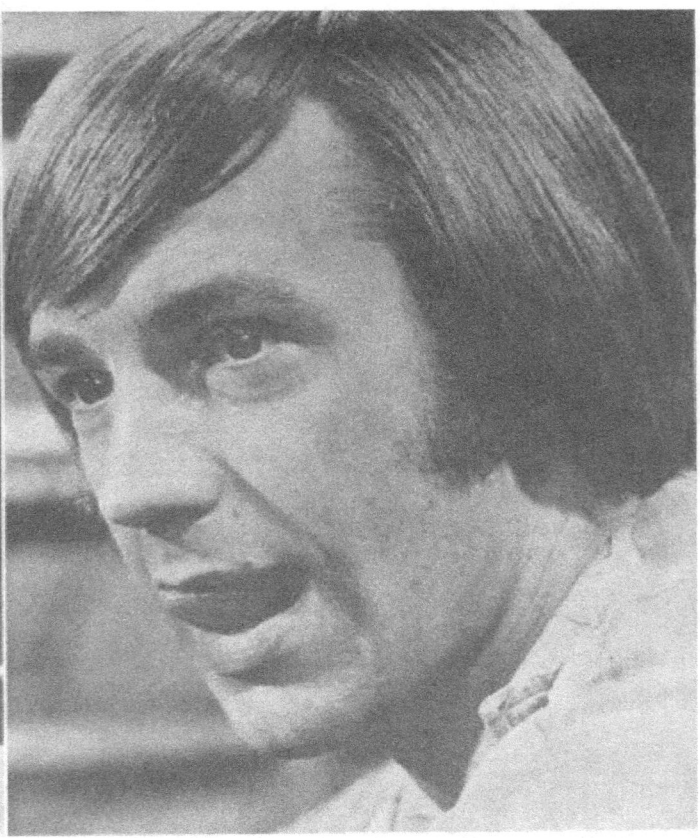

"MONKEES & YOU" BY GLORIA STAVERS

It's flyin' time again — so come along with our editor, Gloria Stavers, as she takes you spinning off into the magic world known as Monkee-land!

WELCOME BACK to Monkee-land! Your host on this trip is Peter Tork, but the very first Monkee you meet is David Jones!

As usual, there is a large crowd of fans standing just outside the North Beachwood Drive entrance to the Screen Gems lot. In the middle of the crowd — all teenage girls, of course — stands the one and only delightful, delicious Davy Jones. Though it is early in the morning and Davy has a hard day's work ahead of him, he has stopped to give autographs and chat with the kids who were kind enough (and lucky enough!) to drop by with the hope of catching him on his way to the studio. When Davy sees you approaching, he recognizes you as a *16* regular and makes his way through the crowd to personally greet you.

"Come along," Davy says, taking your hand. "You're in for the biggest blinking surprise of your life!" — and as you and Davy run past the crowd toward Studio 7, your heart beats a mile-a-minute and you can't help feeling absolutely super. Of all the vast multitude of Monkee fans, *you* are the chosen one who is about to spend untold heavenly hours in the living presence of the four most wonderful guys in the world — Davy, Peter, Micky and Mike!

PETER'S TURN "IN THE BARREL"

In the last issue of *16* you were on hand while Micky directed a *Monkees* segment. Now it is Peter's turn "in the barrel". Peter and Micky are the only two Monkees who want to direct *Monkees* segments, so please don't think that Davy and Mike were left out. They themselves decided to "fade out" when it came to TV directing.

Peter's *Monkees* segment is called *Monkees Mind Their Manor*. The whole thing takes place in merrie olde England. Hold on, me luv — it was actually filmed right on the Screen Gems lot in Hollywood, Calif., but it *looks* as though it was filmed in England. Of course, some of the filming was done at the famous Columbia ranch — and you have the pleasure of watching one of the funniest scenes in the script being shot there. It features an outdoor charity bazaar and there are real tents, balloons, everything — including dart games. Well, there were *supposed* to be dart games, but you have to smother a giggle as you watch the propman running about confiscating the darts from the Monkees — who have been having a ball popping all of the balloons with them!! At one point you, Mike, Davy and Micky really break up as the exasperated propman runs across the field, hands Peter a big bunch of balloons, and says, "O.K., *you're* the boss today. *You* blow 'em up!"

"Wow!" Davy shouts suddenly. "It's raining!"

You start to run for cover, but Mike grabs your hand and says with a slight smile and a Texas drawl, "Don't you know about us movie folks? We don't let nothin' like a little rain bother us."

Before you know it, the huge arc lights are wheeled out and the cameras whirl on as artificial "sunlight" is provided for the Monkees' Charity Bazaar.

TORN APART BY MONKEES!

Suddenly a loud voice booms, "*Lunch break!* Everybody take an hour — Monkees take 45 minutes!"

Mike, the expectant father, wanders off to find a phone;

MONKEES ARCHIVES 3

Davy surrounded by fans at the entrance to the Screen Gems lot.

Super-director Tork at work on the Monkees set.

Micky disappears; and you find yourself standing between Davy and Peter.

"She's mine!" shouts Davy, pulling one of your arms.

"No, no!" cries Peter, pulling the other. "She's mine!"

They look so dead serious that you wonder if they *are* really having an argument over lucky you, or are just gagging around! Whichever is true, you have ascended from Monkee-land to Monkee-*heaven!* After all, it isn't every day that a girl has two of the world's top teen idols quarreling over which one she will lunch with!

"I'll tell you what," Peter says. "I will take this half of her — and you take that half of her."

They earnestly agree, and both boys march off in opposite directions — each holding on to one of your arms! Clowns that they are, just when they've stretched *you* to the breaking point, they swing around and bump smack into one another!

Davy says to Peter, "What on earth are you doing here?"

"I always come here to get out of the rain," Peter explains seriously. "By the way, have you met my girl friend?"

Davy looks you over, shakes your hand and says, "Don't believe so, but she sure looks good to me. Shall we eat *her* for lunch?"

Your private Monkee dreams are suddenly interrupted by the onslaught of a cute little MG driven by a cute little brunette. The car bears right down upon you. The boys hold their ground, and the MG screeches to a halt two inches from Peter's knees!

"Hi, Marilyn, you little daredevil," Peter says calmly. And the boys introduce you to their secretary/Girl Friday, Marilyn Schlossberg. You are delighted by her warmth and friendly manner, and you're grateful to her too — when she suggests that the boys take you off to the ranch cafeteria "... before it is too late to get anything good to eat!"

CONTINUED ON PAGE 36

MONKEES ARCHIVES 3

One of Peter's tasks as director of the segment was to wrap up his buddies and stuff them into coffins.

"Hey, sweetheart...."

One of the funniest scenes in **Monkees Mind Their Manor** features an outdoor charity bazaar.

"MONKEES & YOU"
CONTINUED FROM PAGE 9

MONKEE MUMMIES

Back at Studio 7 that afternoon, fun-time *really* begins! Fun-time for Peter, anyway. One of the jobs of the "director" in *Monkees Mind Their Manor* is to wrap up the other Monkees like mummies and stuff them into coffins! (If you wanna know why — you gotta see the segment!)

Every time Peter gets one Monkee wrapped and encased, the one he completed before pops out of his coffin.

"Hey, sweetheart!" cries Micky, popping out of his wrappings — to Peter's dismay. "Wanna suck blood with me?" Then Micky, who is inclined to crack up at his own jokes, bursts into a powerful, hearty *har-de-har-har-har!*

Somehow, Peter manages to get the scene down without blowing his cool — or his top, for that. However, he does have quite a hassel getting all three of his little friends to stay "wrapped up" and in the coffins — *all at the same time!*

UP IN DAVY'S ROOM

At tea time, Davy comes up to you and says. "How would you like to see my room?"

At first, you are not quite sure what he means, but your answer — without hesitation — is "yes", and Davy escorts you to his brand new, recently decorated dressing room. The first thing that amazes you as you walk in is the "lobby". The lobby is actually a small living room. The door to the left of this room opens into Micky's dressing room, and the door to the right leads to Davy's dressing room. The living room itself is finished in royal blue. It has a color TV set, two overstuffed chairs and a great big couch.

Davy says "hi" to some guys as you fly by and you instantly recognize David Pearl, Neko and some of Davy's other friends. Davy's dressing room features a double-deck sleeping bunk, the top half of which is covered with clothes, photos and copies of *16* and *16 SPEC*. A rack with some of Davy's *achkans* on it stands in the corner and there is a large, colorful *hare krishna* poster on the wall. Davy explains to you, "*Hare krishna* is an ancient chant and the words are whispered softly or thought upon in solitude. They bring a feeling of joy and contentment. We Monkees first learned about *hare krishna* from the Beatles. They had made up a little song using these words and George Harrison taught it to Micky and Micky taught it to us."

MONKEES ARCHIVES 3

"Har-de-har-har-har!"

Trouble at the coffins: "Hey, will you guys please stay wrapped up?!"

The Monkees with Myra De Groot, who plays a fuddy-duddy English schoolteacher in the segment.

Mike and Davy crack up as Peter voices his doubts after his directorial chore is completed: "Hey, man—we think you were great!"

The light on Davy's private phone is constantly blinking and you are both amused and amazed that Davy doesn't even notice it. At last he says, "Oh — *that*. It never stops ringing. It is supposed to be my unlisted, super-private number, but somehow it just leaks out. Well, let's see who it is."

Davy sits down and softly chats for a few moments and you wonder who the lucky listener is. "Nothing exciting," he says when he hangs up. "Just the gardener to tell me that 'Susie,' my dog, dug up three rows of flowers!"

MONKEE "CHIT-CHAT"

After the tea break, it is back to work for the boys. You spend the rest of the afternoon watching them mug through their scenes while Peter keeps a sharp eye on his buddies.

The last shot of the day is a hysterical scene between the boys and Myra De Groot, who plays a fuddy-duddy English schoolteacher named Mary Friar. Super-director Tork is so good that the boys actually get through early and spend the last 30 minutes or so chit-chatting with you. When you ask Peter how he feels after having directed the *Monkees* segment, he thinks for a minute and then says, "Micky was much more radical than I. I used one camera — making master shots and close-ups. Micky did the opposite. I don't know whether the Monkees are hard to direct or whether I am just not experienced enough, but it wasn't easy. Even so, I'm hooked, man. I am really going to try it again. You know what? Now I would like to direct a musical spectacular!"

Mike and Davy, who have been eavesdropping, suddenly crack up. "Hey, man — we think you were great!" they exclaim. And all at once you realize that they are not joking; that they had a ball working with Peter and really *mean* what they said.

Once again a fabulous Monkee-time has come and gone. You are sad because it is over, but you are glad because you know that this is not really the end. There's more — *much more* — to come later.

Yep, that's right! Don't miss the June issue of 16 Magazine and Monkees And You—when Peter, Mike, Micky and Davy invite you to the exclusive preview of their fantastic new Monkee movie! The June issue goes on sale April 25.

"My First Kiss" by Susie Cowsill

Tommy, Susie, Davy & Lauren.

Ten-year-old Susie Cowsill had the thrill of her life! After three years of wishing, she finally got to meet Davy Jones — and he gave her that "unforgettable" first kiss!

IT FINALLY HAPPENED! I really and truly met Davy Jones! I'd been dreaming about it for so long that I still can't believe I really met him! But I did — and *he kissed me too!* Gosh, I'm getting all carried away! Let me tell you all about it from the very beginning. I want you to share my wonderful, exciting experience with me, cos I'm sure that you love Davy just as much as I do!

THE BEGINNING

It all began in September of 1966, when I first started watching *The Monkees* on TV. *The Monkees* was my very favorite TV show, and I immediately got a super-big crush on the Monkee with the adorable English accent. I liked everything about him — the way he looked, the way he walked, the way he sang, the way he danced — and I especially loved that super-sweet smile of his! Just *everything!*

My one wish was to meet him in person, and needless to say — all that I talked about was Davy Jones. I even wrote Davy fan letters. And you know what? Davy *answered* one of my letters! So all of you *16*-ers who write to your favs — *don't give up hope!* I couldn't believe my eyes at first, but there it was in black and white — *a letter to me from Davy Jones!* In his letter, Davy said that he too hoped we could meet someday. That was over a year ago, and we Cowsills were still living in New York City. Davy lived in California. I thought I'd never get to meet him. But I didn't give up wishing and — you guessed it — I didn't give up *talking* about Davy, either!

Time passed and a few months later we Cowsills moved to Santa Monica, California. I must confess, the first thing that popped into my mind when Dad told us we were moving to the West Coast was, *"That's* where Davy lives — maybe I'll get to meet him now!" Well, no such luck! We moved to California last September — almost a year ago — and I had just about given up hope of *ever* meeting Davy when a wonderful thing happened!

ENTER — TOMMY BOYCE

One afternoon, not too long ago, I was sitting in the reception area of our manager's office, waiting for my dad (who was in a meeting with Lenny Stogel, our manager). Suddenly, the front door opened and in walked Tommy Boyce. "Uncle Lenny" (he's really not a relative — but we've adopted him into our family!) also manages Boyce and Hart, and Tommy dropped in to talk some business. Since my dad was with "Uncle Lenny" in his private office, Tommy sat down to wait and we began to chat. Naturally, I got around to discussing Davy Jones. (Davy seems to pop into *all* of my conversations!) Tommy didn't mind talking about Davy, cos they're good friends. Not only do Tommy Boyce and Bobby Hart have an office at Screen Gems, but they wrote and produced many of the Monkees' hit records. After a moment, Tommy looked at me smilingly and said, "Susie, would you like me to introduce you to Davy Jones?"

Well, I just sat there with my mouth wide open — in shock and totally speechless! Finally, I managed to mumble, "C-c-could you — would you *really?*"

Tommy grinned his adorable grin and said, "I *can,* and I certainly *will.* As soon as your dad is finished with his meeting, we'll make all the arrangements — O.K.?"

I don't actually recall what happened after that. It's a good thing my dad was there, cos I was too excited to even remember my own name — let alone any of the details of how, when and where I would meet Davy! However, I do remember asking if my girl friend Lauren could come along too. Lauren is Uncle Lenny's daughter and (naturally) she loves Davy too. So I thought it would be great if Lauren and I met Davy together. Uncle Lenny, Dad and Tommy agreed, and after a long discussion — the plans for my "big day" were all set!

MONKEES ARCHIVES 3

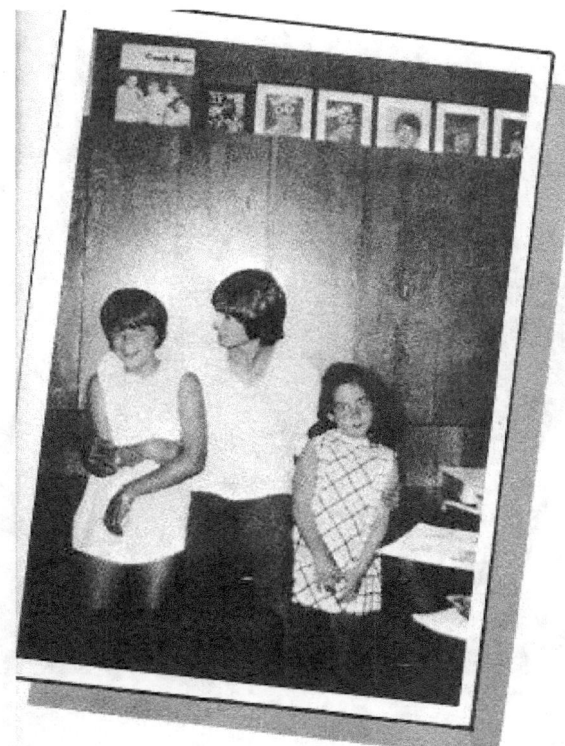

"I almost screamed again!"

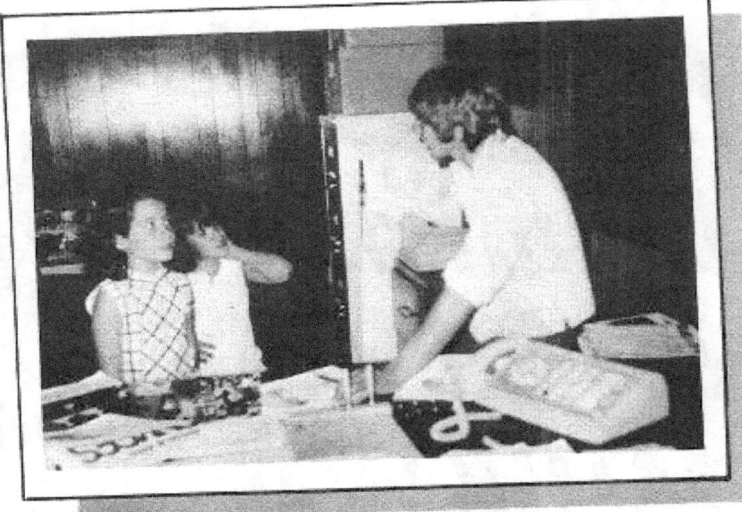

"Davy was so wonderful — I felt that I had known him all my life!"

MORE SURPRISES!

A few days later, Lauren and I were on our way to the Screen Gems offices on Sunset Boulevard in Hollywood. That's not the place where the Monkees' recording studios are. It's the building where all of the Screen Gems executives have their offices — and it was also the place where we were going to meet Davy Jones in person! Once there, Tommy Boyce escorted us into a room, sat us down — and went off to get Davy. To my surprise, I was very calm — or at least I *thought* I was! Suddenly, the door opened and when I looked up — there stood *Micky Dolenz*, grinning and looking just like I'd seen him on TV hundreds of times! Micky winked at us and said, "Davy will be right in."

He had no sooner completed the sentence when, for some reason beyond my control — I let out a gigantic *scream!* Micky laughed and was very understanding. He sat down to talk with Lauren and me — and I managed to get up enough courage to ask him for his autograph.

When Micky left, I really got nervous! It seemed as though hours had passed while Lauren and I waited for Davy to come. Of course, it really hadn't been long at all, but I began to wonder — *What if he doesn't come?* I didn't know what to do, so every ten seconds I would go to the door and look down the hall. *And then I saw him!* Davy Jones — with his dog "Susie" on a leash — was walking toward me! Well, you guessed it! *I didn't want to* — but I screamed again! And then I ran back into the room to wait for Davy — like I was *supposed* to! The next thing I remember was Davy's face smiling down at me and Davy saying, "Hello, Susan".

Somehow, I remembered to introduce Lauren. Davy shook our hands and sat down to chat with Lauren and me. Suddenly, I felt relaxed. Davy was so wonderful. Just like all of you who spent so many Monday nights watching *The Monkees* on TV — I had spent three years wondering what Davy Jones was really like. I don't know why I should have wondered at all, for in real life Davy is just as lovable and nice as I knew he would be. He's kind and considerate, and not at all snobby. While we were sitting there talking, Davy autographed a beautiful drawing of himself and gave it to me. He wrote: *"To Susan — Best wishes and love — Davy Jones"*.

Lauren and I got lots of other goodies too! Davy signed autographs for some of our other girl friends and gave us Monkee LPs and posters. Then he asked me to send him a copy of the Cowsills' itinerary, cos he wants to come and see our show one day. Davy promised to send me a copy of *his* itinerary too!

THE "SPECIAL" GIFT

All at once, Davy looked at his watch. "Gosh, I'm late — I have to go. I'm so sorry," he said.

For a second or two, Lauren and I just stood there — once again speechless. For a minute, I thought I was going to cry — cos I didn't want to see Davy leave. Davy walked to the door, then he suddenly turned and came walking back across the room. And — guess what he did? He leaned down to *kiss* both Lauren and me! Lauren is kind of shy and when Davy bent to kiss her — she turned her head. But I just *stood* there — and guess what? *Davy kissed me — right on the lips!*

I always wondered what my first kiss would be like. I don't have to tell you how wonderful it was. Of course, I never thought it would come from Davy Jones! Now "my first kiss" is even more unforgettable. But more than that, I'll never forget Davy Jones. He's even more wonderful than I ever imagined and, needless to say, I'll always remember that special day when my dream of meeting Davy Jones came true!

MONKEES ARCHIVES 3

"MY Intimate Childhood Pix" by MICKY DOLENZ

PART 4

Psst! The barrel of Mickys shown here was sketched by — but of course! — our own "infant terrible," Frenchy Blanch!

WHEN I LEFT YOU last month, I showed you the crew-cut, brown-haired picture of me that got me my role in **Circus Boy**. Funny thing about TV people — the first thing they did was to **change** me! They let my hair grow out, dyed it blond and switched my last name to Braddock. Here I am with "Chimp", who was on the show with me for two years.

MONKEES ARCHIVES 3

This was taken by my dad in 1955, when we lived on Magnolia treet in North Hollywood. Yep — I used to wear my **Circus Boy** utfit at home. Yep — I did know how to play the guitar, but not ery well. Little did I dream that one day I would be a recording rtist!

Here's a picture of me — "Micky Braddock" of **Circus Boy** — when we were on location. This location happened to be around a swimming pool in Las Vegas. (Doesn't that seem a rather strange place for a circus to pitch tent?)

In 1957 I finished shooting **Circus Boy** and started going to public gh school in Hollywood. Here's a candid of CoCo and me that my om snapped. Don't know whether you can tell it or not, but my air was growing in brown again.

Whew — I made it! At 16, I was graduated from Grant High School in North Hollywood. There were practically no pictures of me taken after this until the time I became a Monkee. However, there were plenty taken of my mom, step-dad and sisters, and I'm going to introduce you to them next month. See you in the October issue of **16**, which goes on sale August 22!

MONKEES ARCHIVES 3

When I was seven and a half, "Mamoo" (my grandma), Mom, Coco and I went to Texas (where this picture was taken) to visit my great-grandmother, Mrs. Nancy Hornby — whom I nicknamed "Gram". She still lives in Austin and watches The Monkees every Monday night.

One day Dad sent me out to rake the leaves. I got the job half-done and settled down for some quiet "gold-bricking", when Dad came out and snapped this picture.

Mom, Coco (at three and a half) and me (almost eight) in our Easter finery. Speaking of good-looking chicks, how about that mom of mine?

You can write to Micky Dolenz at: P.O. Box 1198, Los Gatos, Calif. 95030. Be sure to put "I Am A 16 Reader" on the outside of your envelope.

MONKEES ARCHIVES 3

MONKEES ARCHIVES 3

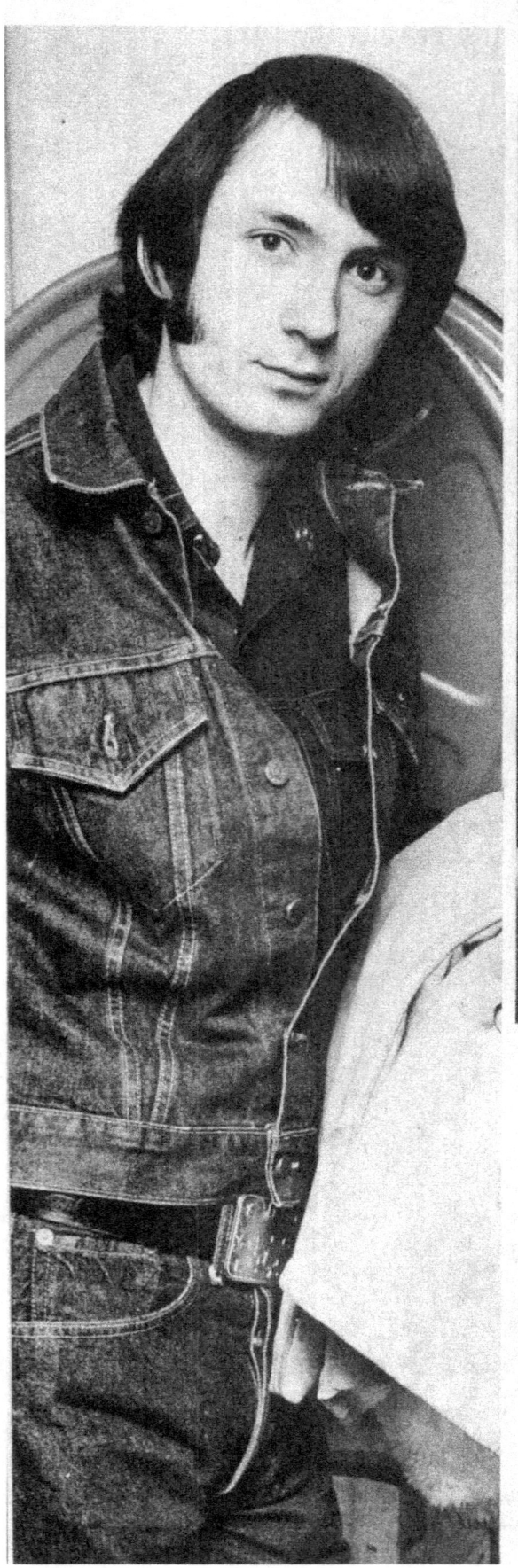

This photo wasn't taken at the recording session which Mike and Phyllis were invited to. This one was taken at an earlier session when the Beatles recorded another track for the same album they recorded the night the Nesmiths visited. But, as you can see, the same informal atmosphere is present.

MONKEE MIKE MEETS THE BEATLES!

MONKEES ARCHIVES 3

If you are lucky enough to be invited for a visit by any of the Beatles — either at home or at the recording studio — you are expected to follow one polite rule: Don't talk about your meeting with them. If you break this rule and talk to others about their private lives, the Beatles simply won't ask you over again.

That is why Monkee Mike Nesmith didn't talk about his two meetings with the Beatles. First, he was invited to one of their very unusual and very private recording sessions. And, then, because he and John became friendly, Mike and Phyllis were invited to spend a weekend at the Lennon's house in Weybridge.

Until now, what went on during those visits between the pop world's greatest super-stars has been a very special secret.

But FLIP was the only magazine in the world at that historic and exciting Beatles recording session which Mike and Phyllis attended, and so we are able to bring you this exclusive story of what actually happened...

MONKEES ARCHIVES 3

Mike got around during his London trip. Before he went to the Beatles recording session, he stopped in to see The Kinks record.

The Complete True Story Because FLIP Was The Only Magazine On The Scene...

At about 10:30 p.m. on a cold and miserable March evening (it was a Friday), Mike and Phyllis were ushered into the vast EMI Abbey Road studios where The Beatles were to record with a 41-piece orchestra.

The scene they came upon was strikingly fantastic. The entire orchestra was decked out in formal evening dress, wearing an assortment of false faces—from huge ears to enormous spectacles to protruding teeth. And George Martin, the Beatles' producer and conductor, was leading the orchestra while balancing an enormous four-foot long false nose.

John Lennon was dressed in his favorite, well-worn green suit; Paul McCartney was wearing a chef's hat and apron (for no apparent reason); George was dressed in white Indian clothes, and Ringo was wearing regular trousers and a jacket. Mick Jagger was wandering around the studio in the company of Marianne Faithfull and Donovan.

Phyllis looked bewildered and kept asking Mike, "What's it all about?" Mike was fascinated by all the surprising happenings and got into a lively discussion with John and Mick about filming techniques. He was told that the Beatles were making a film of themselves making this LP and that most of the fancy dress was because of that.

Mike started looking closer at the things around him—and, like Alice in Wonderland, he found them "curiouser and curiouser." There were water taps fastened to the cellos and double bass, and someone suddenly introduced "Crazy Foam" onto the scene. In a couple of minutes, everyone was splashing the white foam around and people were being dragged through the messy madness.

But there was a record to be cut—and the splashing stopped for a while. The track was "A Day in The Life Of," written, of course, by Paul and John. The introductory bars of the song were played through—in all, it involved maybe 25 seconds of music—and after five or six run-throughs, the incredible session was over!

Meanwhile, more Beatleantics were being filmed by anyone who could pick up a movie camera lying around the studio and shoot scenes. Mick was involved and so was Ringo, the photography buff, who was taking specially angled shots. The musicians took off their jackets and color slides showing weaving colored patterns were projected on their white shirt fronts. Kind of human movie screens!

The cost of the studio and the equipment for the filming on this occasion was estimated to have cost about $10,000—which Paul paid for.

The finale came when the entire

MONKEES ARCHIVES 3

assemble—including Paul and Mike—mounted a rostrum and was asked to sing the notes "E" and "A" for a certain music effect on the record. Manfred Mann's bass player Klaus Voorman (who also designed the Beatles' award-winning "Revolver" album cover) lead the spectacular chorus. And the most expensive and exclusive musical note ever recorded—with contributions from Mike, Mike, Marianne, Donovan as well as the Beatles—was captured forever!

Mike was then asked a series of questions, which he answered in his dry manner. John was asked the same questions and replied in kind. "Yes," he said, "it is all a big scene and I'm full of LSD, cocaine, heroin, and whisky—Goodnight!" Proving, as ever, that John is always most interesting when he is not especially nice.

The next time we looked at the watch it was 2 o'clock in the early morning, and the "Crazy Foam" was all used up. So, the party moved on to the Bag O'Nails Club, which was too crowded, and then on to the Scotch of St. James. Somewhere along the way, Mike and Phyllis detached themselves.

It had been an unbelievable evening for them and they retired to think about it. They were looking forward to the weekend because they had been invited to the Lennon's happy Weybridge home. And John had invited Mike to try some musical experiments on his precious Melotron.

After the recording session and the weekend, reporters kept bugging Mike and Phyllis for details about their experiences with the Beatles and with the Lennons. But Mike, respecting their privacy (as well as his own), said nothing more than, "I liked the Beatles... you know it was groovy...we listened to a lot of good sounds, you know."

But now you **do** know—just a little—because you were there at the Beatles recording session with Monkee Mike and his lovely wife!

Wherever they are, in London or Los Angeles, FLIP is with the Monkees! Our young staff of accurate action reporters covers all their exciting activities as they happen so that you can be there—with Davy, Micky, Peter and Mike—as quickly as we can take their pictures and print their words! Many more on-the-spot scoops will be in next month's issue of FLIP, on sale July 11th!

Here are Mike and Phyllis on their way to The Kinks' recording session. Phyllis enjoyed their very exciting trip, even though at moments it became much more hectic than she could have ever imagined. But she realized that it's all part of being a Monkee's wife. And so she was always cheerful and calm, no matter how mad it got!

MONKEES ARCHIVES 3

HOW DAVY HAS CHANGED

As Told By Marcia Strassman

a (fave) foto feature

Davy and Marcia Strassman have been friends since he played in "Oliver" on Broadway. In this exclusive interview she tells how Davy has become more warm and wonderful in the time between the play and the Monkees' TV show.

(Hey kids, you remember Marcia's hit record "The Flower Children"!)

⬆ Could a girl ask for more? Davy's playing his newest song for me. I can't wait until I hear it on the newest Monkee album. Outasite!

⬆ Pretty soon I got into the act. Davy started teaching me some of the vocal parts of the song and I thought we were great! Hmm, I wonder if we could make a record together. David Jones and Marcia Strassman together. Ah, dreams!

⬆ Here we are outside Davy's new home near the beach. It has room for as many horses as he can want.

⬇ My favorite comedy shot. Davy's always clowning around with his friends. I'm glad I'm one of them.

⬇ Help! Bet you didn't know Davy is a great wrestler, did you? He's unbeaten by anyone his own size.

⬇ We're admiring the flowers in his new yard. Right after this we had the biggest flower fight ever seen!

Turn to Page 60 for Story ➡

HOW DAVY HAS CHANGED

CONT. FROM PAGE 4

●●●●●●●●●●●●●●●
Davy and Marcia Strassman have been friends for many years, from the time when they both lived in New York. Here Marcia tells about her friend, David Jones.
●●●●●●●●●●●●●●●

How did you meet Davy?

I met Davy in New York when he was doing "Oliver!". A very close friend of mine was in the show with David and he introduced us. I was interested in acting, too, and professionally I thought Davy was the best thing in the show. He had a very vibrant personality on stage. We became very good friends then, as close as we are now, and that's why the friendship has kept up.

How has Davy changed since you've known him?

He's always been a very warm, sincere, wonderful human being. Now he's just more and more of these things. He cares more for his fans than anyone else I know and he's always going out of his way to give an autograph or talk to a fan, whenever he gets the opportunity. He's like this with everyone. Once you're David's friend, you're **always** his friend and, even if you haven't seen him for a couple of years, once you see him again it's like you've never been away.

Have you and Davy ever dated?

No, never! David and I are just friends and that's the way it is with everyone. He just doesn't date as such. If you're his friend he'll come over and pick you up and take you to play a game of pool or something but it's not like a date at all. Even in New York I never knew him to date. For one thing he just doesn't have the time because of his career and for another he's not interested in getting tied-down with anyone at the moment. He's friends with everyone but that's as far as it ever goes. He's always sweet and kind, too; he'd never hurt anyone in the world for anything. He's just a true friend to everybody.

MONKEES ARCHIVES 3

HOW I GOT TO KNO[W]

Mike was the first Monkee that I met, way back in early 1964, when we were both going to San Antonio College. In fact, Phyllis went there too and we were very close friends. I can't remember exactly how Mike and I met, but he was fooling around with folk music and so was I. It was like a little community of about twenty people. He used to set up jobs for us and we would work at a bunch of clubs and shopping market openings.

MIKE ACCOMPLISHES

My first impression of Mike was that he was going to be a star. He knew that he would be—he's just that type of person. He has an air about him and when he says something you believe it. I said, "Mike, you can do great things!" and sure enough, he did! In all my relations with Mike, he's always been a guy who accomplished what he wanted to.

We became close while working in these folk clubs. After he came to California we kept in touch, but not often. The next big meeting we had was when he was in his rock and roll group. He was on tour through San Antonio and it was the first time I'd seen him in a couple of years.

He sort of got me interested in coming to California, but it still wasn't something I thought I'd do. He talked about things I would have liked to do, only he really did them! This time he had more ideas and better-laid plans than when he left before and his songs were greatly improved. When he left this time, we kept in fairly close contact.

SCRIPT-WRITER?

While I was at the University of Texas, I got a telegram with Mike's phone number. This was after he had done the Monkees TV pilot. I called and talked to him and he told me that the show was starting up and they were looking for good writers. He said, "You've always come up with good one-line jokes, so why don't you make an attempt at writing something and see if you can get on the writing staff?"

So I whipped up something in a rush, but it was sent back because I'm lousy at writing scripts! But with it came a letter saying "You've got a great sense of humor. Why don't you come out anyway and we'll find you a job somewhere?"

BOTH DAVIDS MEET

So, that I did. I drove out to California in my broken car, which

MONKEES ARCHIVES 3

DAVID PRICE WITH MICKY.

THE MONKEES by David Price

was loaded to the hilt. It died right in front of Mike's house—I just made it up the hill! Of course, with my grand entrance I woke everyone up. Davy was living with them at the time and Mike had gone somewhere. So we sat around and talked for awhile.

Once you get a chance to talk with Davy, he's a fantastically easy person to get to know, very open. He decided to take me on as his buddy. He and Phyllis and I went around Hollywood the next evening and he showed me all the sights. We really had a crazy time!

CLIMB HILLS, MAKE FRIENDS

A few days later, we were at the Troubadour with Mike and he had to leave, so we were left without a car. I had gotten to know Davy, but not really well. It was kind of like two people who just happened to be in the same place.

So, we decided to walk from the club back up to Mike's house. On the way up we got to talking and then I found out what the real Davy Jones is like. He talked about his father and all about his life. I opened up about myself, too, and we ended up huffing and puffing our way up the hill.

By the time we got up to Mike's house, we were great friends and we have been ever since. In the next few days, it seemed that everyone had picked a stand-in except Davy and he said "You're it!" So, I was!

MEETING MICKY

Micky and I met about a week later at a party. He impressed me as a very funny guy with a great sense of humor. It's always impressed me about Mike that you can give him an object and he can talk about it for thirty minutes. Well, Micky can do the same thing.

When we met, I thought "What a clown!" and I can sure see where he got the job. He was a groovy guy but he moved and thought lightning-fast! I could never stop him long enough to get into a serious conversation.

But now I've known him for quite awhile and he's slowed down a bit. I've been able to learn what he's really like inside. I now know him as a very deep thinker, who is concerned with people and very involved with the love movement.

BREAKING THE ICE

Peter and I didn't meet until the show started. When I first came out here I was very quiet and I didn't say much. I guess I was kind of dazzled by all the excitement, straight from Texas and working on a TV show. Strangely enough, we got to know each other because of this very reason.

Peter is one who does not speak unless he has something to say. So we spent several months not saying **anything** to each other. We sort of drifted together to find out why neither of us was saying anything and once we started talking—wham!—we couldn't stop! He's very philosophical and so am I. I majored in philosophy in college, so we found we are very much alike. Now we're really great friends.

It's groovy getting to know the Monkees and even groovier being friends with them. I've learned from our friendship. I have things in common with each of them, yet they're all such individuals, that each one has something special and unique to offer. It's fun and rewarding to find out just what that special something is!

MONKEES ARCHIVES 3

DAVY JONES: MR. BIG HEARTED

By Neko Chohlis, Davy's Close Friend

Whether he's doing a concert, a Monkee segment, a recording session or greeting fans—wherever he goes Davy gives every ounce of himself as a performer and as a person. That's why he is called "Mr. Bighearted".

To Davy, show business is a business. It's his job and he gives it everything he's got—even if it means getting a little scared once in awhile. Sometimes I look at him before a concert—where the kids are really going crazy—and he has a slightly panicked look on his face.

Once the audience was even throwing things, and there were four big holes in the screen that we showed slides on, right behind the Monkees. But Davy just stood there, smiling and dodging things and singing away.

He loves doing concerts and approaches each one in an open-minded way. I've never heard him complain about doing a concert. You can tell by the way he performs that he digs it. He knows exactly what the audience wants, and he really grooves with them.

AWARE OF FANS

To Davy, the more people, the better! His fans mean so much to him that he wants to give them everything they came for. He delivers the best show he can by really communicating with his audience—kneeling down, pointing to them or blowing a kiss. He can feel the warm vibrations coming from the audience and that makes him perform even better.

In fact, he's the most fan-conscious performer I've ever seen. He realizes that if they get carried away, it's done out of love and enthusiasm. He feels he owes them a lot of thanks so he always does things to make them a little happier.

Like, when we were in Detroit, there was a girl in a wheel chair. I went back to get Davy's autograph for her since he was her favorite Monkee and I told him about her. She was sitting right by the edge of the stage, so when Davy went on to sing, he came over to her, kneeled down and sang to her for a few minutes. He's always doing little things like that.

Continued on page 20

MONKEES ARCHIVES 3

MONKEES ARCHIVES 3

DAVY JONES: MR. BIGHEARTED
cont. from page 18

BROADWAY BITS

Davy also lets his love for the theater shine through on his solo numbers. He sticks in a bit of Broadway when he sings "Gonna Build Me A Mountain" and he loves to dance. He puts extra little bits into his act to make it super-special, because Davy's an actor and a dancer as much as he is a singer. In fact, he digs acting best of all.

Before a concert, Davy, like the other Monkees, sits around and does nothing until right before he goes on stage. Then the four guys get in a football-type huddle. Each puts one arm around the next guy and puts his free hand on the stack in the middle of the huddle. Then they mumble **"Hare Krishna Rama, Ha-ba-re-ba-so-bo-see-ben"** or some nonsense thing like that. It's just a little ritual that ties them all together into a closer group so they'll groove with each other.

RECORD SESSIONS

Before a recording session, Davy will come in and joke with the people who are there. If he's in an extra-groovy mood, he'll clown around through the whole session and make crazy facial expressions while he sings.

Davy's always livening up everyone around him. And when he gets together with Micky while they're recording, it's one big comedy show!

Recently Davy has gotten involved in song-writing—constantly sitting down at the piano or trying to figure out a tune on the guitar. The only thing he doesn't like about the recording part of it is that the four Monkees can't record enough **together** because each one has so many things happening every day. On a given day Davy may be the only one at the studio.

GIVES HIS HEART

As for filming the show, sometimes he gets tired. But a true pro like Davy keeps going and never lets on. When the Monkees began, it **could** have become a drag because they just memorized scripts and repeated the same thing over and over.

But now they ad-lib. Davy just looks over the script, then forgets the lines and says it in his own words. It's a lot more fun for him that way!

Davy really loves being a performer and sincerely wants to give everyone watching a part of himself. He's all heart and that is why he will always be a successful entertainer and a successful human being.

MONKEES ARCHIVES 3

THE REAL SCOOP
What it's like to work with the Monkees!

What are Davy, Micky, Peter and Mike really like when they're slaving away under the hot lights on the Monkee Set?

Do they put-on the stage crew, the actors and extras? Or, do the Monkees bend over backwards to help others?

For the first time, here is the behind-the-scenes story of the award-winning comedians, as told by one of their prettiest leading ladies.

by DONNA LOREN

MEETING DAVY AGAIN was a big thrill for me. We had worked together two years before on "Shindig" and then I remember thinking Davy would be a big star someday. One thing's for sure... Davy hasn't changed a bit since I met him. He's still the same sweet boy he was when we met. During the breaks between scenes, Davy and I talked about horses a lot. Davy's crazy about them and so am I. He still thinks he would like to be a jockey. I don't think he'll ever get the chance because he'll always act.

MONKEES ARCHIVES 3

DAVY MADE IT FUN to do all the scenes. This episode will be shown in October and we got to wear beautiful costumes. I played a harem girl and Davy took the part of a shiek. He really looked the part, too. There was one scene where the camera used the speed-up action that is so characteristic of the show. It was fun because I got to tell Davy how groovy I thought he was in the show and that's really the way I feel about him when we're not play acting. Right after I finished this part, the word came that I was to go to Europe and do some special appearances. This really thrilled me. The Monkees seemed to be a good luck charm for me.

A KISS FROM DAVY is fun in any girl's estimation. I was surprised about the professional way all the Monkees act toward their work. Everyone of them made me feel right at home and did everything he could to make the work fun.

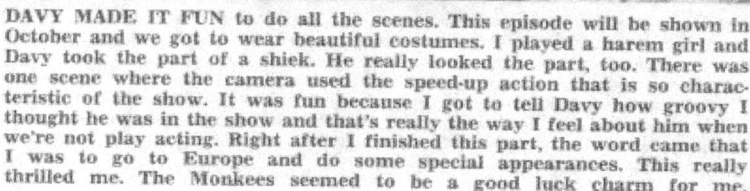

PETER is sweet. He likes to talk about lots of other things besides show business. When he isn't in front of the cameras, Peter spends most of the time in his dressing room. He is quite serious minded and keeps informed on what's happening all over the world.

MICKY was in a funny mood most of the time during the shooting. He had been staying up late at night working on some sculpture. He explained to me that when an idea hit him he just couldn't wait to get at it so even if it took him all night, once he started, he had to finish. Mike has a dry sense of humor. When I first met him, I didn't really know whether he was making fun of me by some of the things he said or just being funny. I discovered that his way is just like this and he turned out to be very friendly and quite unusual.

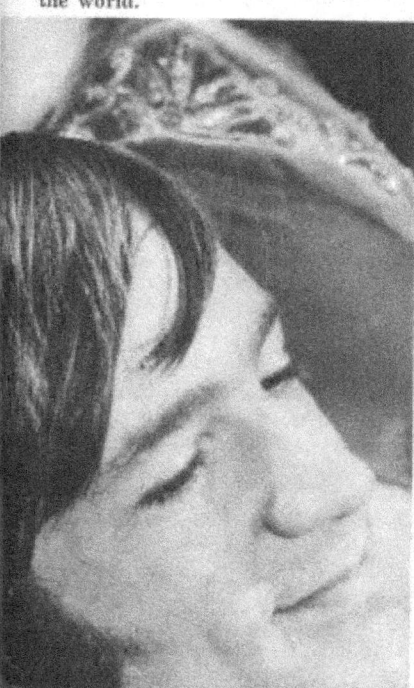

MONKEES ARCHIVES 3

THE MONKEES MEET
MICKY D. TELLS WHAT IT WAS LIKE TO MEET PAUL McC. !

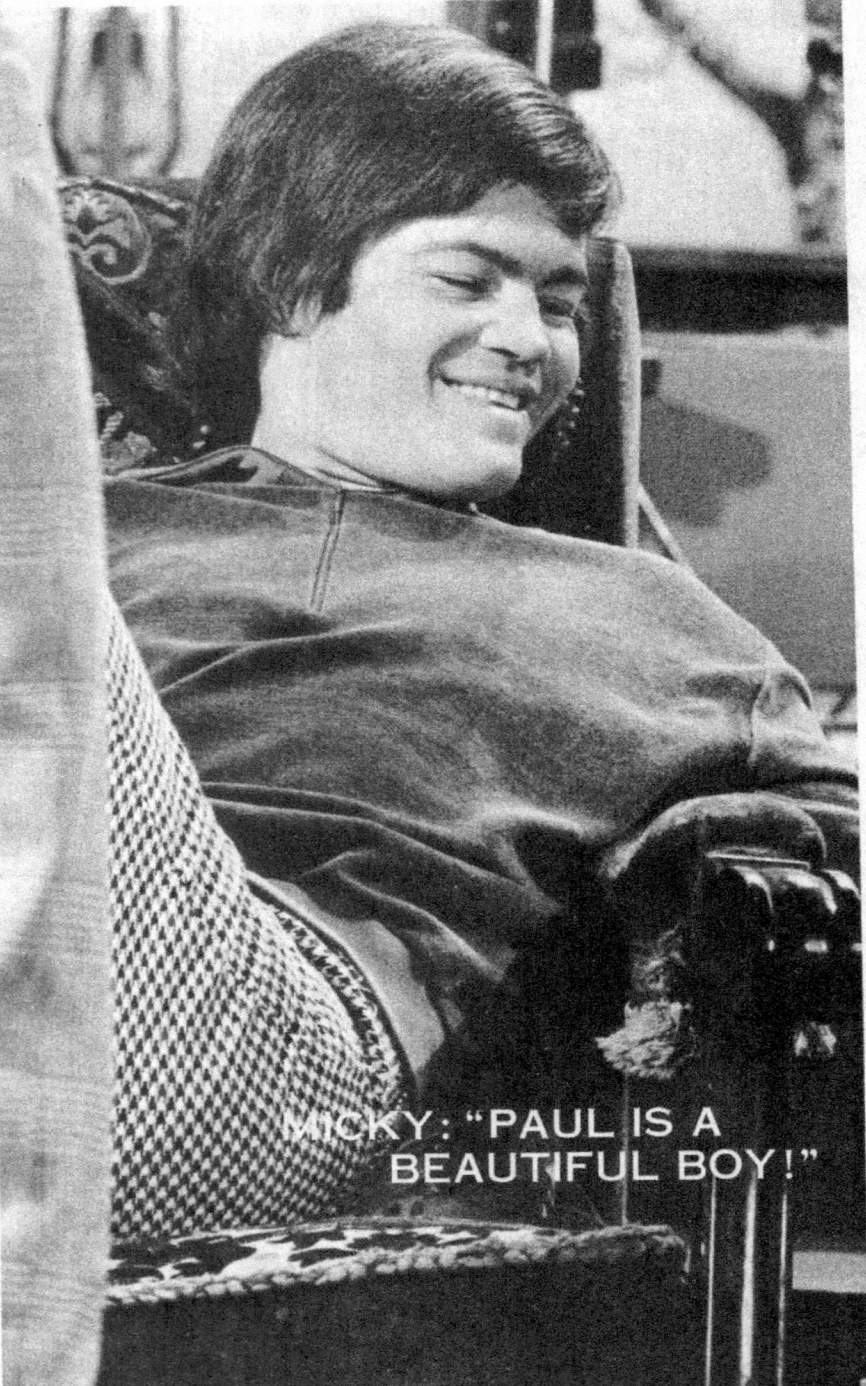

MICKY: "PAUL IS A BEAUTIFUL BOY!"

Micky Monkee meets Paul McCartney!

That was the exciting pop surprise which happened at Paul's St. John Wood's home when Micky visited London.

Micky had once said that "meeting a Beatle would be rather like seeing God!" But he had an entirely different impression after coming away from his chat with Paul (which he relayed to me during a quick flip in and out of a London TV studio).

"Paul turned out to be a tremendously real and likeable person," he said. "He said that he watched and enjoyed our TV show and that he liked our records. That I think is a tremendous tribute. I expected to be overawed by him — but he's such a relaxed friendly person that I felt completely at ease.

"The Beatles have always been revered by us as a group and there isn't a person on the pop scene who has not been influenced by them but that does not mean we have tried to imitate them on film. Our humor is based upon the type of comedy the Marx Brothers had in their early films.

"Paul is a beautiful guy — his moustache knocked me out — I may grow one like that some day and he wore the most fantastic tie. He asked me if I wanted to drink and I had an orange juice.

"Originally the whole thing was set up as a publicity thing and although I didn't dig that idea much I was really pleased that it worked out so well and that we seemed to get on well together.

"Most of the evening we sat around talking about just everything and he played me "Penny Lane" and some of the tracks off the new LP like "When I Was '64" which is fantastic old jazz type number."

Paul, ever the Beatles

MONKEES ARCHIVES 3

THE BEATLES!

diplomat, had obviously completely won over Mickey and any skeptical opinions he might have had were completely eliminated.

"Micky knows what its all about," says Paul, "I fully expect the Monkees to go from strength to strength. This is no here today and gone tomorrow group. The Monkees are going to surprise everyone."

The little resentment which still exists in British pop circles over the Monkees taking over from English groups seems to be dying and it is quite certain that the cordial meeting Paul and Micky have helped put millions of minds at rest.

Paul once said to me: "When you are young and you are new and you are a big attraction it is inevitable that comparisons will be made between you and established artists — no matter how original you are but eventually, if you have talent, the individuals come through."

Paul was then talking about the Beatles but he might well have been referring to the Monkees.

Paul knows that as the Monkees today are being compared to the Beatles, one day another group will be compared to the Monkees.

And, in their short surprise meeting, Paul gave Micky an idea of what that day will be like.

PAUL: "MICKY KNOWS WHAT IT'S ALL ABOUT!"

MONKEES ARCHIVES 3

MONKEE REFLECTIONS -- PART ONE

(The Monkees have been with us for nearly two super-years now. A lot has happened to them—and to all of us—during that period. We asked Carol Deck, FLIP's Hollywood Editor, who has been close to the group, to tell us how each of them has changed, if at all, during these twenty-two months. This is the first part of her exclusive report. Next month: Mike and Davy.)

PETER: "CHANGED THE MOST!"

Peter Tork is probably the Monkee who's been through the most changes since the group started. When the Monkees were first introduced to the press and public many months ago Peter seemed very much like a squirrel, with bright curious eyes and a sense of eagerness about him, like he couldn't wait to see how it would all turn out.

But then as things began to get going and more and more demands were made on him and on his time, he began to look around and he didn't always seem to like what he saw. The group was constantly being knocked by members of other groups as being a manufactured, no-talent group. And the character Peter portrayed on TV was built up as a simple, rather dumb but well meaning guy and people began to think that this was what Peter Tork was really like.

Peter did some soul searching, trying to find out who he was and how he fit into the whole scene of things, and often during this period of re-adjustment he may have looked a little self-centered, but it was just that he had to go inside himself to find out what he was all about.

This was a rough time for Peter—he was working hard and becoming really successfully for the first time in his life, yet he wasn't sure that the whole thing wasn't going to destroy him emotionally.

But Peter passed that period, came to terms with himself and the people around him and came out the groovy guy he is today. His curiosity about things outside himself has returned and once again he's like a bright, curious squirrel, but a much wiser squirrel now. What he went through was the "Who am I?" phase that almost everyone goes through at one point in his life. It was just that Peter had to go through it in front of millions of people.

But Peter Tork today is quite a guy—curious, peace-loving, interested in different types of religion, particularly the Far Eastern ones, trying different kinds of diets in his attempts to keep in excellent physical condition, reading everything he can get his hands on, learning to tell when a girl likes him for himself or just because he's a Monkee, and most of all, finding peace within himself.

Peter's gone through some rough times emotionally, but he's learned and profited from it and is ready now to cope with the world and with being a Monkee—one of the roughest jobs in the world.

MONKEES ARCHIVES 3

MONKEE REFLECTIONS -- PART TWO
MICKY: "ALWAYS HAPPY!"

The one overwhelming quality that's made Micky Dolenz what he is today is his sense of humor. He has been the clown of the Monkees since the group started and despite increased responsibilities and pressures, he's managed to maintain that humor and use it to the advantage of the entire group.

From the very beginning it was Micky who could take the tenseness out of any situation with just one remark. When the others would begin to slip into cynicism and sarcasm, Micky would come bouncing in with just one incredibly funny remark and everyone would relax and laugh.

In the beginning Micky, like all the guys, had no idea how successful the group could be, so he just lived each day for itself and told himself that if it all died tomorrow at least he would have had fun while it lasted.

But as it became obvious that they were going to make it, it also became harder to keep up a sense of fun when most of the time it was just plain hard work. It became harder to laugh at the little mistakes that caused delays in filming when the little mistakes happened every day and often turned into major mistakes.

But somehow through it all Micky had maintained the sense of fun. Now success has brought him the money to buy many of the things he's always wanted and to do many of the things he's always wanted to do, but success can't spoil Micky Dolenz because he still knows what happiness is. You won't find him trying to buy happiness—he's had it all along.

Sure he can buy fancy cars and gadgets and luxuries, but it still takes very little to make Micky happy—just the bright smile of a fan will do it—and this is what makes him one of the grooviest people around today.

This is Micky Dolenz today—accepting the responsibilities that have been thrust upon him, trying many different things to broaden his interests and his world, digging the simple things in life — smiles and sunshine and flowers and friendship— and above all, keeping a sense of fun about everything he does.

MONKEES ARCHIVES 3

MIKE shares a very private mood with you!

Music is the most important professional part of Mike Nesmith's life—second only to Phyllis, Christian and Jonathan. Mike takes all of his music very seriously, especially when he is listening to it. In this series of exclusive pics, you are with Mike as he listens to some music in the personal privacy of his den.

Sitting on a piece of furniture, Mike seems to be very wrapped up in the sounds which are coming out of his very elaborate hi-fi system.

Guitar at his side, Mike sinks into his sofa, sipping a Coke while letting the music entertain him. Mike's den, by the way, is a fantastic room—complete with a bubble chair which has speakers for the music built in!

Has the music put Mike to sleep?

MONKEES ARCHIVES 3

"COME ALONG WITH ME AS I TRAVEL WITH THE MONKEES!" By RIC KLEIN

Ric Klein is Micky Dolenz' best friend, and, served as the Stage Manager of The Monkees' tour. He is also Micky's stand-in, and the best of friends with Peter, Mike and Davy. Ric kept a day-by-day diary of everything the boys did, and he took hundreds of pics! Ric invites you to join him as he travels, talks and lives with The Monkees! It's a once-in-a-dreamtime adventure only in FLIP!

YOU'RE IN THE PICTURE as Micky, Davy, Peter and Mike take you on tour with them! Your groovy guide is Ric Klein, and the once-in-a-lifetime trip starts right here...

MONKEES ARCHIVES 3

MY DAILY DIARY OF THE MONKEES TOUR!
By RIC KLEIN

One of the show-stopping moments of The Monkees' fantastic stage show was Micky's wild, wild solo spectacular! And, night after night, FLIP's own Ric Klein (Micky's best friend and Stage Manager of the entire tour) had the best seat in the world to watch Micky's frantic performance! Here, in an exclusive series of breath-taking, stop-action photographs, you're on stage with Micky as he flips through his incredible performance!

MONKEES ARCHIVES 3

SUNDAY/NEW YORK

Last month, you lived with Davy, Micky, Peter and Mike as they traveled between Paris, London, New York, Atlanta, Jacksonville, Miami Beach, Charlotte and New York again. And I left off here—on the first Sunday in New York—promising to continue my exclusive day-by-day FLIP diary of The Monkees' Tour. On this Sunday night, we played the last of our three New York concerts. As the first two, it went off perfectly. All the concerts were at the beautiful Forest Hills Stadium, where the national tennis championships are held. And Davy, soccer scrambler that he is, couldn't resist kicking the ball around on the lush green turf. Until the tennis people, worried about their expensive grass, gently asked him to save his soccer for another place.

RIC'S EXCLUSIVE COVERAGE OF THE MONKEES TOUR CONTINUES ON PAGE 53!

MONKEES ARCHIVES 3

MY DAILY DIARY OF THE MONKEES TOUR!

By RIC KLEIN

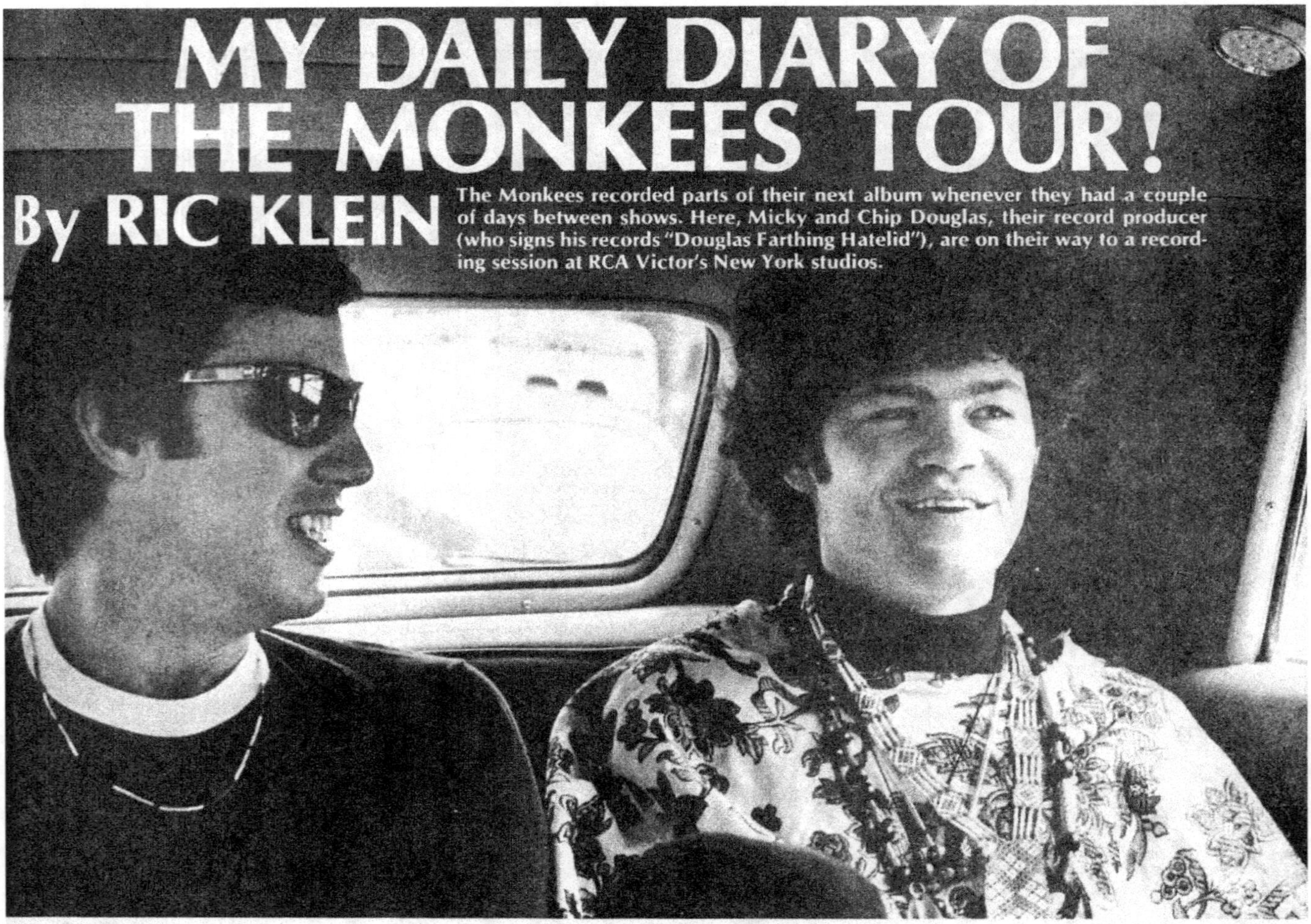

The Monkees recorded parts of their next album whenever they had a couple of days between shows. Here, Micky and Chip Douglas, their record producer (who signs his records "Douglas Farthing Hatelid"), are on their way to a recording session at RCA Victor's New York studios.

MONDAY/NEW YORK

From today until Wednesday, the boys really had time off, time to do most whatever they wanted. The Jimi Hendrix Experience, which was on the tour along with Lynne Randall and The Sundowners, quit the tour here in New York. They felt that concert tours weren't their bag, they wanted to play clubs and develop in other areas. The guys were sorry to see them leave, but nobody was signed to replace them.

WEDNESDAY/NEW YORK

Davy spent some time with Dino Danelli of The Young Rascals. They are each others' best fans. The Warwick Hotel on West 54th Street in Manhattan continued to be our headquarters, and we always had a reception of fans when we entered or left the hotel. And, then, it was time to leave for Buffalo.

Micky cheerfully listening to a playback of something they just recorded. Looks like it sounds pretty good, judging from Micky's happy face!

MONKEES ARCHIVES 3

and flew right out to Cincinnati.

FRIDAY/CINCINNATI

On the flight between Rochester and Cincinnati, we all got into a tremendous pillow fight! Micky, Davy, myself, David Pearl and The Sundowners were in it, and Micky won! He got us all pinned into the back of the plane, he piled up all the pillows and attacked us at will! Don't ever get into a pillow fight with Micky unless you're ready for all sorts of surprises! When we landed in Cincinnati, pillows and all, about 1500 fans were waiting for us. And the trip from the airport into the city was like a wonderful parade, with about 100 cars following us in!

And it was here in Cincinnati that Peter scared the heck out of me! I was in the hospitality suite at the hotel, when I looked out the window! And there was Peter, grinning his grin, standing outside the window! On a one-foot-wide ledge! Eight floors up, Peter had climbed out of his room, and walked the thin ledge on the outside of the building to pull this super stunt! I was speechless, and Peter was laughing at my shocked reaction. I didn't think of it then, but I should have said, "Cats have nine lives, not Monkees!"

SUNDAY/CHICAGO

Micky, Davy, Peter and Mike set a record here! Almost 19,000 people showed up for the concert at the Stadium, which set the record for the largest indoor crowd ever to attend a concert! We stayed at the Astor Tower Hotel, which only has complete suites rather than single rooms. So, each of the boys had a bedroom, living room, sitting room and foyer complex to himself! In the mood for groovy, spectacular living, they visited the "Playboy" Mansion, which is owned by High Hefner, the Publisher of that famous magazine. All of them were there at least once, in this spectacular showplace which has to be seen to be believed, and Peter went back a few times to go swimming while Davy enjoyed the pool table there, and returned for a couple of rounds of friendly pool.

Because of the difficulties in the two cities, we postponed our Detroit concert and cancelled our Milwaukee concert, which had been scheduled to follow our Chicago visit.

The boys now had enough time in Chicago to film some of the "romp" singing sequences for this season's shows, and we took advantage of the extra time to complete several of the musical numbers for the shows you'll be seeing the next couple of weeks.

Nick and Beth Tork, Peter's brother and sister-in-law, met us in Chicago, and decided to travel with us for the remainder of the tour. Peter, who's very close to Nick, was very happy that they could make it.

In Chicago, Micky and Davy also went to the famous Museum of Science and Industry. And they were both flipped out when they went

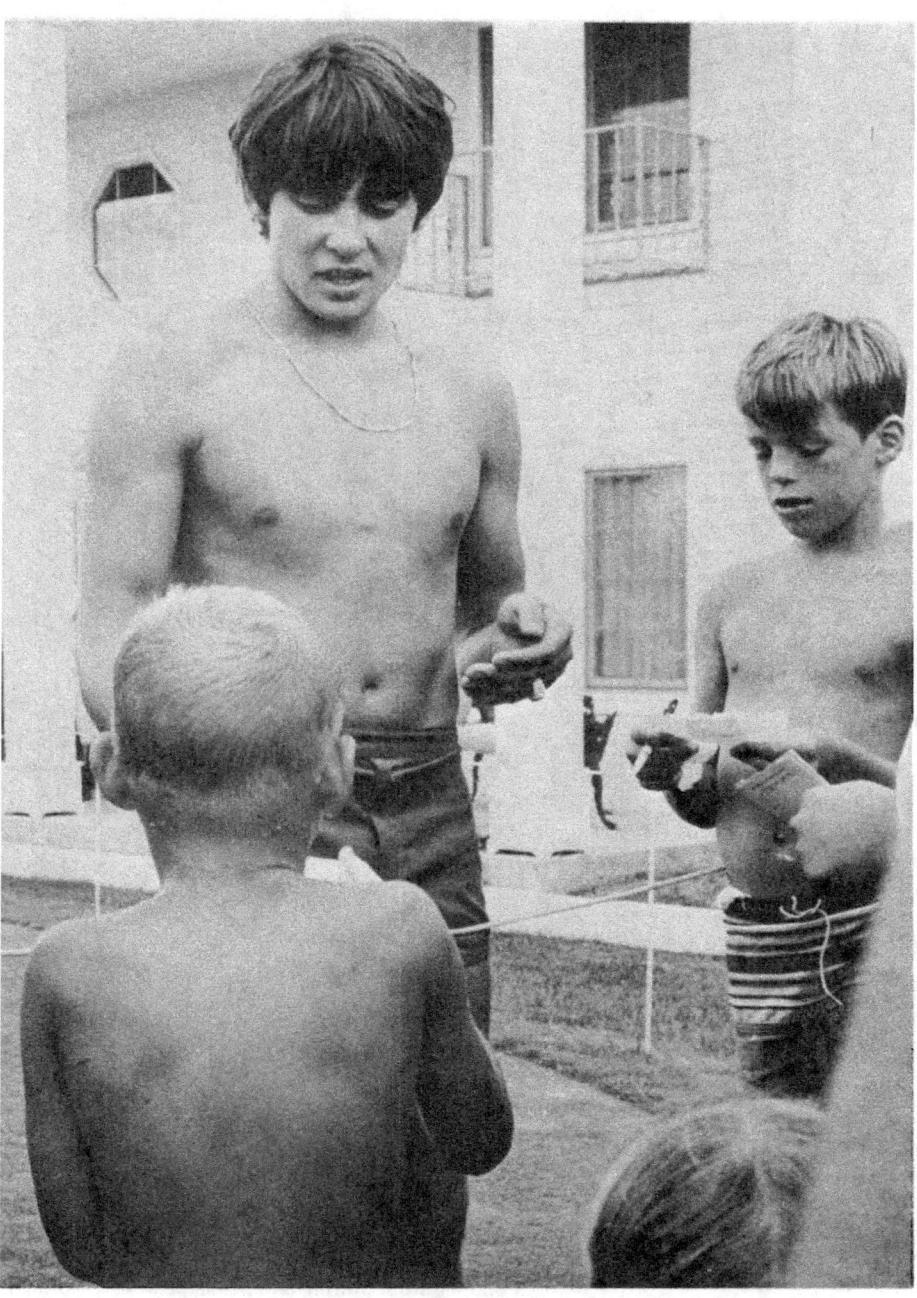

As always, when he had the time, Davy obliges his fans with some prized autographs.

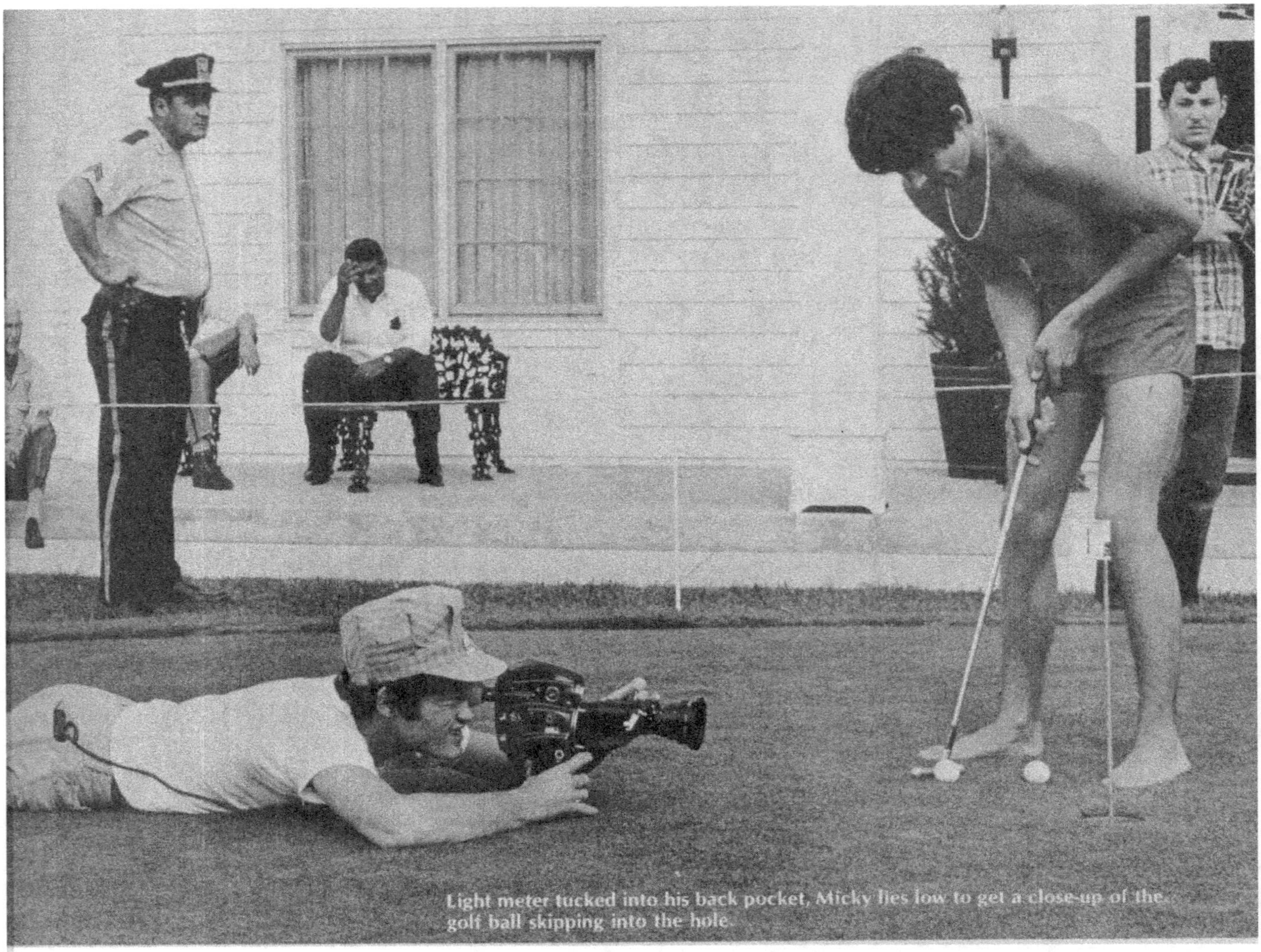

MONKEES ARCHIVES 3

Light meter tucked into his back pocket, Micky lies low to get a close-up of the golf ball skipping into the hole.

into a real coal mine and saw the historic German U-boats from World War Two. They were sorry that they didn't have more time to spend there, and both hope to get back and spend more time in that exciting museum.

FRIDAY & SATURDAY/ST. PAUL & ST. LOUIS

Here, as in most of the cities we visited, Micky, Mike, Peter and Davy went to the local radio stations to be disj jockeys for a while. Micky and Mike are especially good at being DJs. Micky wanted to be a disc jockey once, and Peter may have been one for a short time in his crowded life, during which he's done so many different things.

SUNDAY/DES MOINES

Most of the day was spent lazying around the hotel, Johnny & Kay's. Davy spent most of the day on the putting green, and Micky spent most of the day shooting some 16 mm film. So, I did the natural thing: I took out my FLIP camera and spent most of the day taking pics of Micky taking pics of Davy putting! I don't know if that makes any sense, but I hope that the pics I did do!

WEDNESDAY/DALLAS

I'll pick up here in next month's FLIP, which will be on sale November 9th. What a time we had in Dallas, Mike's part of the world! Dallas and a lot of other surprises will be yours as you continue to travel with Davy, Mike, Micky and Peter in the next outasite issue of FLIP! We'll be waiting for you, so make a date to join us! You'll have the truest and grooviest Monkee seat in the world!

Poooped from putting and posing, Davy takes five on the motel lawn, grabbing a little more sun for his great tan!

MONKEES ARCHIVES 3

MIKE NESMITH'S ACTION ANSWERS!

WHAT DO YOU THINK OF CLOTHES?
"They are very necessary. I take great pride in designing some of Phyliss' wardrobe, and even greater pride in the fact that she makes anything I do design look great."

WHAT DO YOU THINK OF THE MONKEES' HUMOR?
"I'm very proud of the fact that The Monkees have evolved a special humor of their own for the show. I sat for an hour once trying to think of something funny to do with a telephone! Some of Micky's spontaneous actions on the set are in the Marx Brothers class."

HOW DO YOU FEEL ABOUT THE ROLLING STONES?
"What they did to Jagger and Richard over that drug charge in England did almost as much for the cause of reforming out-moded law as Joan of Arc did for Christianity."

HOW DID YOU BECOME A MONKEE?
"I got my job in The Monkees because I'm a con man from way back. You've got to know how to 'shuck'—it's lesson number one. Presenting yourself in the most favorable light."

WHAT DO YOU THINK OF BEATLE JOHN LENNON?
"People are frightened of his apparent scorn, but it's only a defense to hide his real compassion."

WHY DO YOU FLIP OVER GADGETS?
"I'm push-button-made. Always in search of the perfect machine. I guess that's why I have seven cars and everything in my house is gadgets. I can open the doors to our house by pushing a button in the car miles away!"

WHAT DO YOU THINK OF YOUR FANS?
"I like my one!"

MIKE WILL BE BACK NEXT MONTH WITH MORE EXCLUSIVE ACTION ANSWERS! RESERVE YOUR MAD MARCH FLIP NOW! ON SALE JANUARY 9TH!

MONKEES ARCHIVES 3

DAVY FLIPS OUT!

Last issue, Davy played "Words!" with FLIP's groovy Keith Altham. This month, Davy and Keith are back — with the second part of their happy game! Keith tossed words at Davy, and Davy tossed back whatever came into his mind.

MONKEES ARCHIVES 3

MIKE NESMITH—"Skinny The Schneid, who calls me 'Limey The Lip!'"

TUBBY THE PINEAPPLE—"Chip Douglas."

FLOWER CHILDREN—"Nice. I like flowers."

BRITISH PRESS—"Good. Sympathetic. Not out to put you down."

CHARLIE CHAPLIN—"I saw 'Countess From Hong Kong,' which he directed, on my flight over to England. It was just as good with the sound on as off—which must prove something."

POLICE—"Not good enough."

DECOYS—"I hate to see them getting hurt. I wish people wouldn't use them. You can get torn apart looking like any of us!"

THE CHILDREN—"My first venture to record. They made a record for Davy Jones Enterprises. I don't want to stick labels on them"

ANTHONY NEWLEY—"I like 'Roar of The Greasepaint" and 'Build A Mountain,' which I've done in our act."

DAVID WAGSTAFF—"He's a footballer. I trained with him for six months when he came to LA with the Wolves football team. We used to play at Openshow Boys School together."

TENNIS—"A lot of balls."

DAVY JONES—"...and the dulcimer..."

MORE ON DAVY—AND ALL THE MONKEES—IN THE MAD MARCH ISSUE OF FLIP ON SALE JANUARY 9TH! THE GROOVY WAY TO START THE NEW YEAR!

WHAT'S HAPPENING WITH THE MONKEES!
BY RIC KLEIN

A Last-Minute Report of All The Monkees Action!

A lot happens to Micky, Peter, Davy and Mike every month! I am lucky enough to be on the scene as it happens because of the groovy job I have: As Micky's stand-in and as the Stage Manager of their in-person shows.

And, from now on, in every issue of FLIP, I'll be right here to tell you about everything that The Monkees did, are currently doing and hope to do in the future.

The boys have been very active this month.

Micky bought a gyro-copter, which is a one-man helicopter. He's in process of assembling it right now. In his living room!

Micky also bought a Moog Synthesizer, which is a device which can theoretically duplicate any sound in the universe. It's a keyboard, not tuned to any scale, and three other units that resemble a large telephone switchboard. He used it on one of The Monkees' more recent recording sessions.

Micky has just completed putting an eight-foot high redwood fence around the house, complete with electronically-controlled gates. His downstairs recording studio is just about completed. The carpeting has just been put in (even around the columns in the room), and now Micky is waiting for his eight-track tape deck. And, as I am writing this, Micky is thinking of going to Mexico City next weekend for the Mexican Grand Prix. He wants to shoot the race with his 16 mm. movie camera.

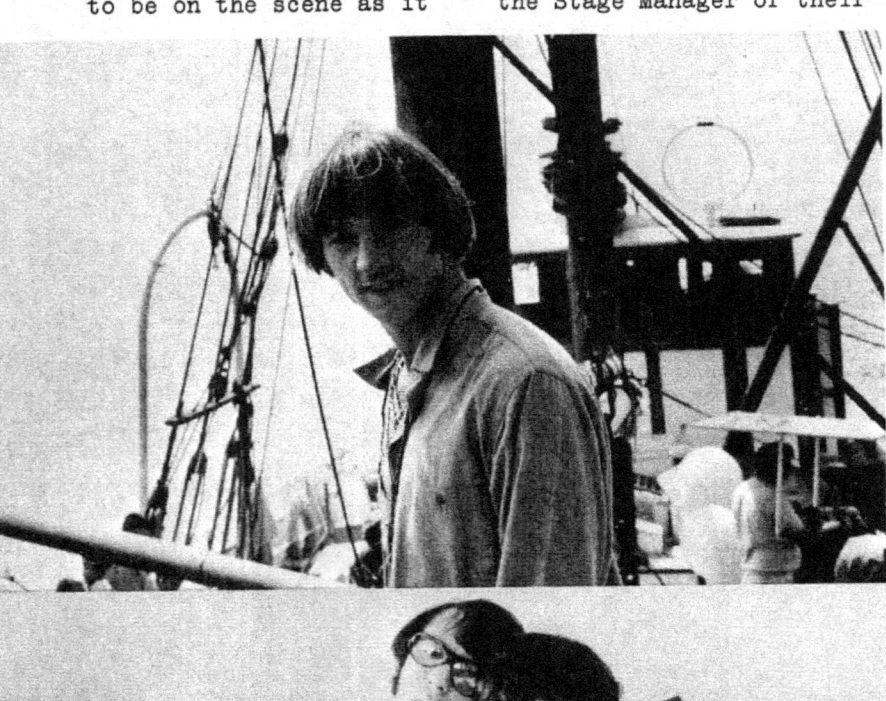

Davy is selling his house in the Hollywood Hills because he bought a 17-acre ranch in Malibu. The ranch has a guest house, indoor swimming pool, and stables. Davy wants to buy some horses as soon as he moves in.

His store in Greenwich Village, which is called "Zilch," has just opened in Greenwich Village in New York City. It's on Thompson Street, and its main thing will be Indian Robes, East Indian clothes.

MONKEES ARCHIVES 3

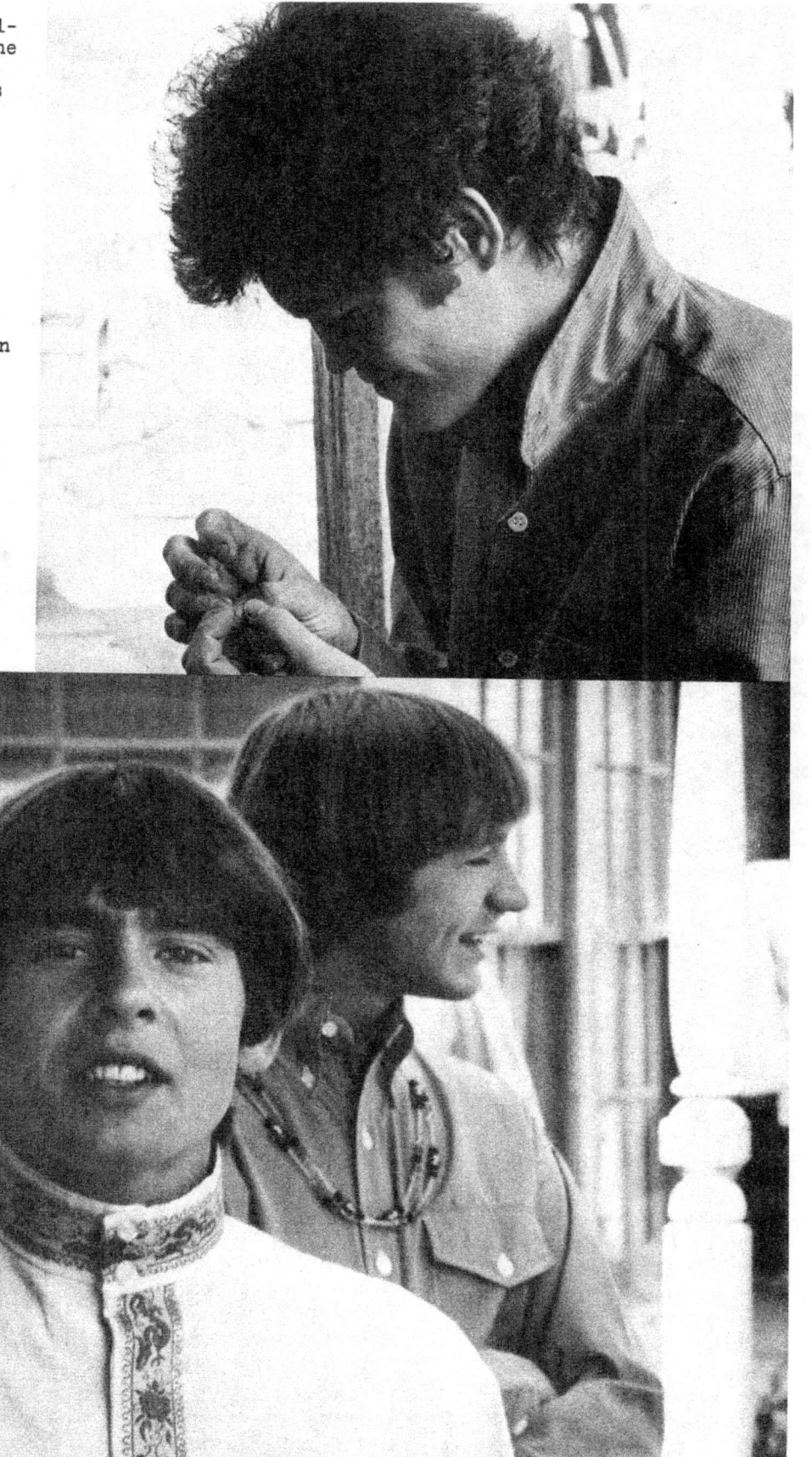

Mike bought a new Cadillac limousine, and had the whole car pinstripped in white and all the windows tinted black. He and Phyllis are waiting for their new home to get finished, and also for their baby, which is expected around Christmas. They still haven't come up with names for Christians's new brother or sister.

Peter is looking for a new house, and he has been spending a great deal of time with The Buffalo Springfield.

And, finally, I forgot to mention that Davy has taken out Sally Field, "The Flying Nun," a few times.

That's what's been happening with The Monkees this month.

See you next month. In the issue of FLIP out January 9th.

MONKEES ARCHIVES 3

"My First Impressions Of The Monkees!" By Stu Phillips

THE COMPOSER-CONDUCTOR OF ALL THE BACKGROUND MUSIC ON THE SHOW!

Stu thinks Davy is the greatest!

Stu at work: composing and conducting Monkees music!

Among the lucky people behind the scenes who work with the Monkees is Stu Phillips, a young New Yorker who composes and conducts all of the background music for the Monkees' show, except of course the Monkees' own records which are played during the show.

Stu is no newcomer to music. He's been composing, arranging, producing and performing for quite a while. His credits include The Hollyridge Strings' Beatles Songbook albums (Vol. 1, 2, and 3), the "Stu Phillips Presents the Monkees Songbook" album by the Golden Gate Strings and several hit singles including "Johnny Angel" by Shelley Fabares, "Goodbye Cruel World" by James Darren and "My Dad" by Paul Peterson.

But Stu is now midway into his second season of doing all the background music for the Monkees and here he tells FLIP of his first impressions of Davy, Micky, Mike and Peter.

"Let me start with Davy, since he's the one I know best. When I first met him, over a year ago, I first noticed the following things: he was prompt, on time and he worked very hard, he was very pleasant and very easy to get along with. And all of that really did surprise me, 'cause at that time I wouldn't have been the least little bit amazed if he'd been like an hour late and bugged and above everything. But instead he was very pleasant and easy to work with. He worked, got his stuff done and left.

"This was on the episode last year when Davy was supposed to become the biggest singer in the country and have the number, one, two and three songs in the nation all at the same time. I had to write the lyrics for the songs for Davy and each one was supposed to be the same song upside down or backwards or something.

"They all had to sound the same. So the number one song was "I really love you, I really love you, I really love you, really I do" and the number two was "Really I love you, really I love you, really I love you, I do really love you" and number three was "I really, really, really love you, really, really,

MONKEES ARCHIVES 3

really love you, really, really, really love you, really I do." It was funny idea and I think it came off well. That was the first time I really worked closely with David.

"Mike I met when he was Michael Blessing. I was at Colpix Records and so was he. My first impression of him was that he was weird, really weird. As Michael Blessing he wanted to revolutionize the world. In fact the first record he put out was a big protest song. He was a very strange, far-out boy.

"And Micky, as far as I'm concerned, has always been a doll, a real great guy. I first met him too last year on the Monkee set when we had some preproduction things we had to work

Stu knew Mike when he was "Michael Blessing!"

Stu's 4-year-old daughter will never forget Micky!

out. He's a lot of fun, a lot of laughs, and always has been, as long I've known him. He's just a lot of fun, nothing's too serious with him. I guess if you know him really well, there probably is a serious side to him, but mostly he's just a lot of fun, real camp.

"I took my daughter, who's four years old, on the set one day to meet the guys and Micky stopped right in the middle of filming and took pictures of her and Davy together and then said 'Alright, Davy, now you take pictures of me and her together.' He made a really big deal out of it and he didn't have to do it.

I guess I really like Micky because he's very unpretentious but he likes to put everyone on. He loves to be funny.

And Peter I really don't know very well. I personally admire him on the shows because he's learned an awful lot since he started and I think he's progressed into quite a good actor. I don't really know him well but he strikes me as nice."

Needless to say, Stu is now one of the Monkees biggest fans. He's one of the lucky people who gets to work for them and you can bet he really loves his work!

Stu hopes to get to know Peter better.

MONKEES ARCHIVES 3

DINNER WITH THE MONKEES!
(But, Who's Eating?)

The Grammy Awards, the Academy Awards of the recording industry, are awarded each spring at four dinners around the country. This year, the dinners were in New York, Nashville, Chicago and Los Angeles. FLIP was at all of 'em, but probably the grooviest place to be was at the Century Plaza Hotel in Los Angeles—because that's where The Monkees were! And, as this pic proves, madness reigns wherever Davy, Mike, Peter and Micky are! Micky and Mike were quietly eating dinner, when along came the Jones boy to shake up their appetite!

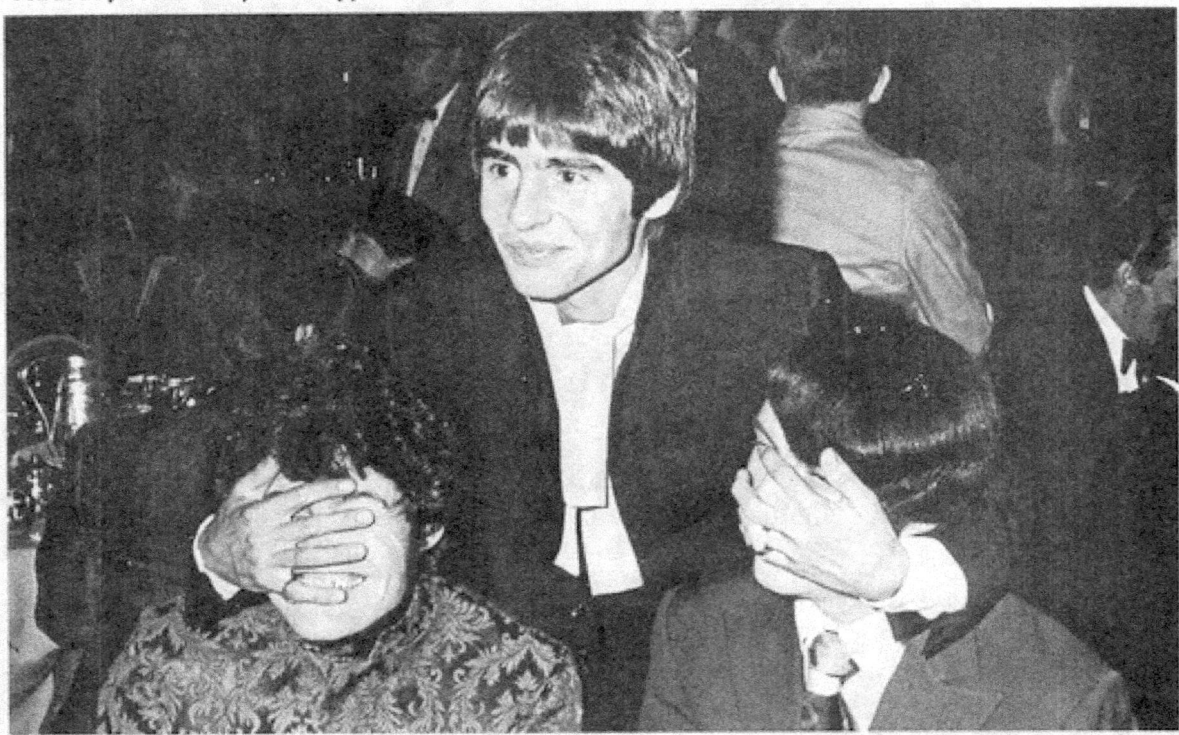

After his grand entrance, Davy joined the others already at the table (that's Samantha Juste next to him) and tried to eat dinner in between all the fans, well-wishers and reporters who stopped by.

MONKEES ARCHIVES 3

Samantha looks radiant and Micky animatedly gets into a wide-eyed conversation.

Here, Mike joins Micky in sharing a happy moment at the exciting dinner.

Exclusive FLIP Photos By Erik Whitaker

There were so many awards, you couldn't tell the players without a scorecard! Mike and Micky check out all the nominees—including a group called The Monkees!

MONKEES ARCHIVES 3

YOUR MONKEES MOVIE PREVIEW!

A tight close-up of Mike in his Army outfit.

"SGT." MIKE NESMITH CLOSE-UP!

Like any combat-weary soldier, Mike takes a mid-battlefield break.

Off the set, Mike talks about the movie with a reporter.

Looks like Mike managed to take off his fatigues without rattling his sun-glasses, which haven't budged!

MONKEES ARCHIVES 3

MONKEES ARCHIVES 3

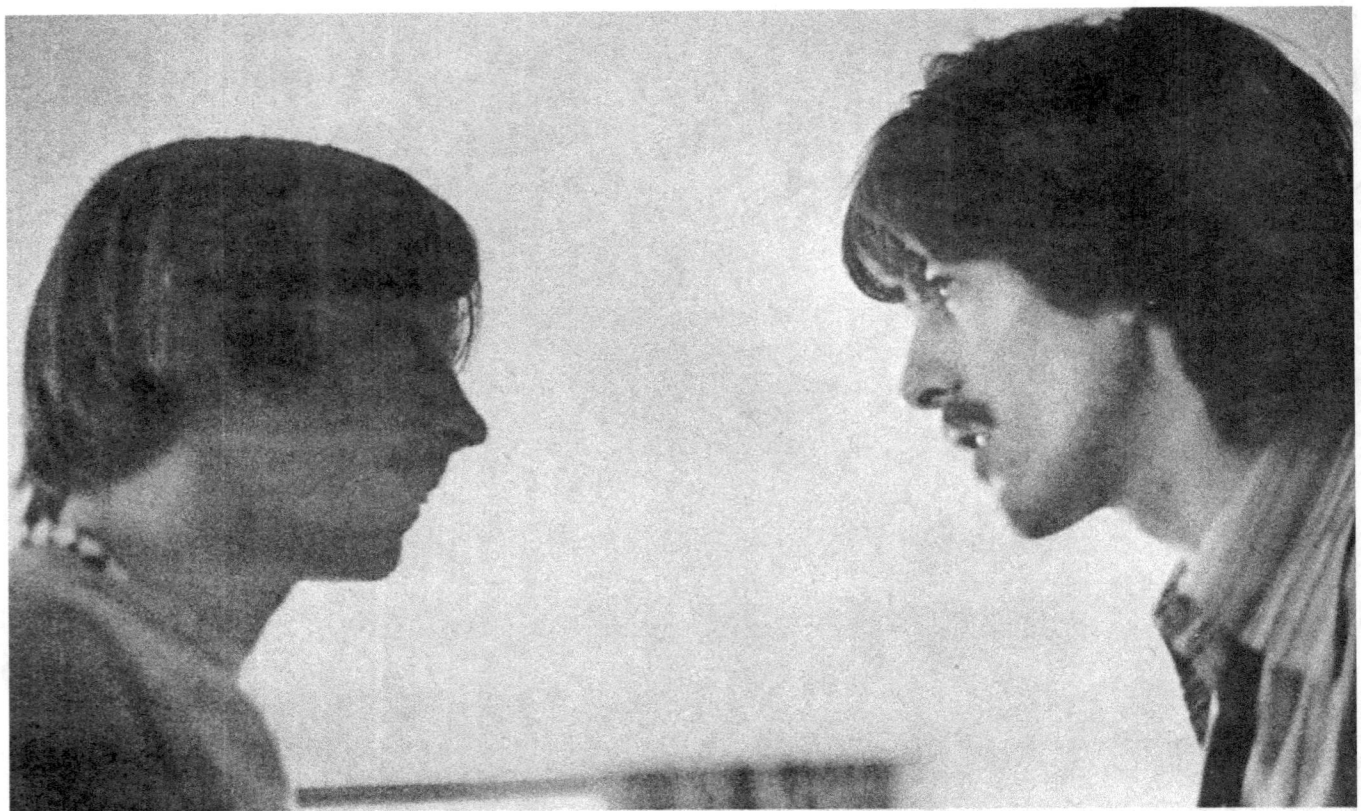

Peter and George Harrison face-to-face. Peter happily accepted George's invitation to come by the house while he was in London.

MY DAILY DIARY OF THE MONKEES TOUR!
By RIC KLEIN

WEDNESDAY/PARIS

After five days in Paris, which were exciting and interesting and included a three-hour traffic jam The Monkees created, we left for London at 10:30 in the evening on Air France flight #860. The tour officially started in London, where we did five concerts. We landed in London at 11:35 p.m., but the airport was crowded with fans even though it was nearly midnight. We were all very tired, so we went directly to our hotel (the Royal Gardens) to get some sleep.

THURSDAY/LONDON

Micky, Davy, Mike and Peter slept late. But they had to be at Wembley, the stadium where they were doing their concerts, at 1 o'clock for a rehearsal. They made it, and went through the rehearsal, which lasted two hours, with The Epifocal Phringe and Lulu, who were appearing on the show with them. After the rehearsal, the boys had a press conference (they only held two all summer—this one in London and another in New York). Then, everyone went back to the hotel. There were crowds in Kensington Park, across the street from the Royal Gardens Hotel, day and night, all the time The Monkees were in London. And the boys made very frequent appearances. Mike was staying in room #551, Davy had #550, Micky had #547 and Peter was in #546. Davy's old-time friends, Basil and Boots, came to the hotel and he spent the evening

MONKEES ARCHIVES 3

SUNDAY/LONDON

Two concerts at Wembley again today. Spencer Davis and his wife Pauline and Keith Moon of "The Who" were there, and spent some time with us. Mike was so exhausted that he almost passed out during the concert. Mike and Micky went to The Speakeasy again, and Davy went there as well as to the Cromwellian, another club. We used to race our limousines through London, getting our chauffeurs to beat the others (we rode in separate limos). They were wild, wild races, but our driver was the wildest of them all! Late in the evening, we all went to a party at Robbin Alan's, which lasted until dawn.

MONDAY/LONDON

Davy went up north today to see his father. Micky and Sam went shopping. Mike went to Radford to pick up his new super-mini car. And Peter stayed in the hotel for most of the day. That night, NEMS held a party at The Speakeasy for The Monkees. George Harrison, Paul McCartney, John Lennon, Jeff Beck, Keith Moon (of The Who) and Eric Clapton (of The Cream) were some of the groovy people at the party. After the party was over, Micky went for a walk in Kensington Park.

TUESDAY/LONDON

Micky went to Kensington Park, where he sang to a crowd of about 400 surprised and happy girls. He stayed until 2 o'clock, and then went shopping with Samantha. Davy returned from the north, after spending two days with his Dad. Phyllis flew in, and Mike took her driving in his new mini (which only broke down once!!).

WEDNESDAY/LONDON

Mike bought a Mercedes 600, and then spent the evening at The Speakeasy with John Lennon. Peter spent the day with George Harrison and Ringo. At George's house, Peter and George exchanged thoughts on the sitar and got along like old friends. Micky and Davy went shopping. It was their last night in London, and they all went to a dinner party at the Speakeasy before getting some sleep before their flight to New York.

THURSDAY/NEW YORK

It was 11 o'clock in London when the boys boarded their jet for New York. But it was only 6 a.m. in New

Peter pointing something out to Ric, who's taking the pic. That's Jimi Hendrix next to Peter on board the 58-foot yacht they spent some time on in Miami.

Micky gags it up for Ric's see-all camera!

Davy taking it easy on board the luxurious yacht.

MONKEES ARCHIVES 3

You probably couldn't catch it from your seat, but Mike was actually smiling on stage!

MY DAILY DIARY OF THE MONKEES TOUR!

This is what it would have looked like if you'd been able to get this close to Micky during a show!

York. This upsidedown time made it possible for them to have a press conference in New York the same afternoon. Fans were waiting at The Warwick Hotel in Manhattan, and the boys sat on their second floor window ledge, their legs dangling, talking to them before and after their hectic press conference. New York was only a stopover for the press conference, with nothing much scheduled. And, after a day during which they crossed the ocean and added six hours to an already busy day, they just wanted to take it easy and get to bed early.

FRIDAY/JACKSONVILLE

The boys left New York in their own plane, a groovy DC-8 which had The Monkees symbol on the outside and was fabulously comfortable on the inside. Because of the tremendous amount of equipment they need for each concert, a second plane goes along just to haul the equipment. It's a C-46 cargo model, and we took turns flying in it (because it was considerably less comfortable than the DC-8, which came complete with mini-skirted stewardess). We arrived in Jacksonville about 4, went swimming at our motel (The Heart of Jacksonville Motel) and then went to bed early.

SATURDAY/JACKSONVILLE

The concert was at 8, and we stayed around the motel for most of the day. After the concert we left for Miami.

SUNDAY/MIAMI

We goofed around the pool of the Eden Roc Hotel for most of the day, splashing, getting splashed and getting sun. The concert was at Convention Hall in the evening, after which we returned to the hotel. A couple of the guys went to a few nightclubs.

MONDAY/MIAMI

We all slept late, and then went for a groovy boat trip out in the Atlantic Ocean. It was a 58-foot yacht, and I took lots of pics. Lyn Randall, the girl on the show, The Sundowners and Jimi Hendrix all came along for the happy ride. Afterwards, we still found some time to swim at the pool. All of which made us late for our flight to Charlotte, N. C.

TUESDAY/CHARLOTTE

A quiet day at the Red Carpet Inn, with the concert at 8 o'clock in the Coliseum. Afterwards, we left for Greensboro, N. C. by bus because it was so close.

WEDNESDAY/GREENSBORO

Spent the day at The Oaks Motel, where The Monkees spent lots of time at the pool with many fans. After the concert, we flew to New York. A word here about all the traveling: It's very complicated,

MONKEES ARCHIVES 3

and for the purposes of the official schedule, there was a personnel code which listed us under our Code Numbers rather than our names — making scheduling easier. Micky was given number 1, Peter had number 2, Mike had number 3, Davy had number 4, and I had number 10. But the numbers were chosen at random (the producers of the show, Bert Schneider and Bob Rafelson, had numbers 24 and 25 — out of 27 possible numbers).

THURSDAY/NEW YORK

Arrived at 1:30 in the morning, direct from the Greensboro concert. Stayed at the Hotel Warwick, where fans were waiting when we arrived in the middle of the night. Peter had lunch with his grandmother and Mike saw some relatives during the day. Davy went sightseeing and Micky went to see the hit Broadway show, "Mame." Then we had dinner at the Voisin Restaurant before getting back to the Warwick. Micky, however, left again to visit The Electric Circus, a wild new discotheque-type club which had just opened in the East Village.

Peter's banjo was one of the highlights of each show!

FLIP's Ric Klein had the best seat in the house for every Monkees concert! He was the stage manager for the entire tour, grabbing exclusive and groovy pics of The Monkees in action! Here is Davy in a remarkable close-up of his on-stage performance!

FRIDAY/NEW YORK

It was a quiet, private day. Mike and Peter basically stayed at the hotel while Davy and Micky went out on a number of personal visits. One of the few real off days of the entire summer, with not even a rehearsal scheduled. But there was a concert at Forest Hills in the evening, the first of three concerts in New York.

SATURDAY/NEW YORK

After the second New York show, all of the boys followed Micky's path and visited the way-out Electric Circus. Micky first had dinner at "Tortilla Flats" in the Village with Steve Sills of The Buffalo Springfield.

SUNDAY/NEW YORK

This is the exciting day where I'll pick up my personal diary of everything that happened on The Monkees tour. So very much happened, that I'm sure that you'll want to reserve your copy today of the next outasite issue of FLIP. It'll be on sale October 10th, when I'll be back with more of the private, personal and true experiences I shared with Davy, Micky, Mike and Peter!

MONKEES ARCHIVES 3

"I'm Ric Klein, And I Lived With The Monkees On Their Tour! "Starting Right Now, I'll Share Every Groovy And True Monkee Happening With You!"

Ric Klein is Micky Dolenz' best friend, and served as the Stage Manager of the entire Monkees tour. He is also Micky's stand-in, and the best of friends with Peter, Mike and Davy. Ric covered every spectacular second of The Monkees Tour exclusively for FLIP! He kept a day-by-day diary of everything the boys did, and he took hundreds of candid pictures. This once-in-a-lifetime scoop starts on the very next page of this issue of fab FLIP!

MONKEES ARCHIVES 3

"MY DIARY OF DAVY JONES' EARLY DAYS!" By Linda Joyce Miller

Linda Joyce knew Davy when he lived in New York and was starring on Broadway in "Oliver!" They often saw one another, and Linda kept a diary of all these events. Now that Davy is one of the world's greatest super-stars, these early happenings take on a very special and important meaning. In this issue and in future issues of FLIP, Linda will share them with you.

Last issue, I told you some stories of David's kicky sense of humor long before he ever thought of becoming a Monkee. There's one I forgot about. Once, during the finale of "Oliver," the audience could faintly hear the words of The Beatles' song "Twist and Shout" coming from the stage. Instead of singing the closing song, David had decided to change the script slightly!

Here are some more personal memories of David during his New York days...

A TEABAG SITUATION

From Linda Joyce's collection of early photos of Davy comes this one of him backstage, looking surprised but happy.

One afternoon, after a matinee performance of "Oliver," David and I went to one of his "haunts," the Paramount Coffee Shop. He and I sat down at the counter, and he ordered a cup of tea. When his tea arrived, David tapped the waiter and said, "I don't like your tea...it's not as good as ours, y'know." "Well, David," answered the waiter, "what can I tell you?"

David proceeded to dunk the tea bag, and soon there was tea all over the cup, the saucer and the counter! Deciding the tea was dark enough, David picked up the tea bag, held it high up, quietly said "Here goes!" to me, and splashed it on the counter. Everyone looked surprised, but he just put his best innocent look which said, "Oh, my, it must have slipped!" But nobody really minded. Even then, David had that certain something.

"YOU'RE ALL WET!"

"David, help me!" cried out one of the boys in "Oliver!" As he turned around to see what was the matter, water sprayed David in the face. There was a water pistol fight going on backstage, so "our hero" grabbed a water pistol and squirted back with all he had! In the process, he got quite a few innocent bystanders and fans soaked! He loved the water pistol fights, and probably started as many as he ended.

MONKEES ARCHIVES 3

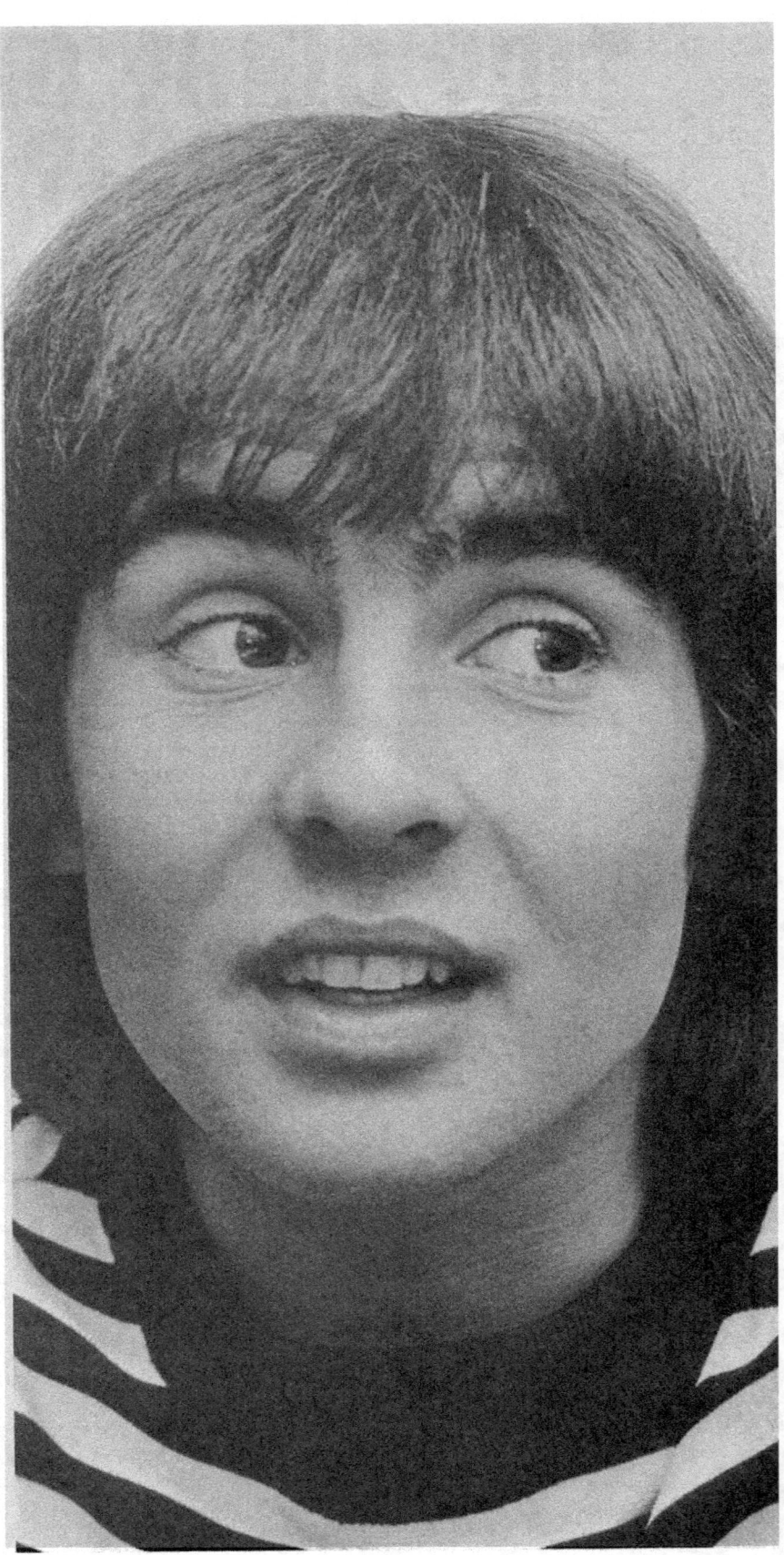

THE UPSIDE-DOWN AUTOGRAPH

"I can't come out dressed like this," David replied to a group of fans one day. As it was, he had only his slacks (knickers) and a little vest on, and he was clearly embarrassed. They kept on asking for his autograph, so he sent a friend to the stage door to get their autograph books. He signed the books upside-down (which is British for Good Luck) and then asked his friend to give the autograph books back to the girls. His buddy couldn't understand why David didn't want to be seen, and So, blushing a bright red, David went to the door himself, mumbled an embarrassed "here y'are," stuck his hand out the door, almost dropped the books, and ran backstage!

DAVID'S PRE-MONKEE RECORDS

After my first story in FLIP, you wrote me a lot of letters (which I'm still trying to answer) asking all sorts of questions about David. One of the questions which kept coming up was what records, if any, David had recorded before he became a Monkee. The facts are that David recorded three single records and one album.

The singles were: (1) Dream Girl/Take Me to Paradise, (2) What Are We Going to Do/This Bouquet, (3) Girl from Chelsea/Theme For a New Love.

The album was called "David Jones," and included these songs: What Are We Going to Do/Maybe It's Because I'm a Londoner/Put Me Amongst The Girls/Any Old Iron/Theme For a New Love/It Ain't Me, Babe/Face Up To It/Dream Girl/Baby, It's Me/My Dad and This Bouquet. The album was half pop songs and half show-type tunes.

MORE NEXT ISSUE

It's happened again! I'm out of space for this month. But I'll have more answers to your questions about David in the next outasite issue of FLIP. It will be on sale September 7th. See you then.

MONKEES ARCHIVES 3

MONKEES ARCHIVES 3

THE MONTEREY

CAROL DECK REPORTS ON A MAD, MAD WEEKEND OF MONKEES, BEATLES AND THE GROOVIEST GROUPS IN THE WORLD!

hard, uncomfortable metal folding chairs. And what a groovy time we had!

Over 30 of the top groups in the recording industry performed, and many more came to see or to introduce friends.

MONKEES PETER TORK and MICKY DOLENZ, though busy recording and preparing for their tour, took time off to come up from Hollywood... MICKY never did make it on stage, except to sit on the side and watch the BUFFALO SPRINGFIELD... but PETER was kept busy all weekend introducing LOU RAWLS and THE BUFFALO SPRINGFIELD and then trying to quiet fans who had climbed up on the walls and roofs of the arena looking for BEATLES.

Rumors whipped around the festival all weekend that at least one, if not three, of the BEATLES were there ...only one not reported seen was RINGO STARR...but none of them ever appeared on stage ...Heaviest rumor was that GEORGE HARRISON would introduce RAVI SHANKAR, who completely creamed everyone with his very peaceful, beautiful, refreshing music... but GEORGE never showed.

MICKY DOLENZ was far from inconspicious in his complete (American) Indian outfit, including feathered headress which flowed down to his heels... MICKY told FLIP that he made the entire outfit himself and that the head-dress, despite its size, was really very light and comfortable... but he did have to take it off when he went out into the audience to watch the WHO because people couldn't see over it.

At one point MICKY couldn't find a seat and decided to sit on the ground in an aisle but told he would have to clear the aisle, so he returned backstage where he spent most of the festival.

Another who made no attempt to remain unnoticed was Rolling Stone BRIAN JONES, who strolled about during the entire festival in floor length (India) Indian beige robes ...Brian looked very pale and his hair seems to be a lighter shade of blond...he could definitely use a little of the good California sunshine ...unfortunately he didn't get any in Monterey where it was cold and overcast the entire weekend and even rained once while OTIS REDDING was on stage.

Photographers at the festival didn't

MONKEES ARCHIVES 3

POP FESTIVAL!

Photos by Robert W. Young

give BRIAN JONES too much trouble until PETER TORK decided to say hello ...PETER walked across the front of the arena and leaned over to shake hands with BRIAN, he was sitting in the second row with a blond girl who was with him all weekend, and several dozen flash bulbs exploded in their faces.

At one point later a photographer was giving BRIAN a particular;y bad time and an official asked him to move on and offered to throw him out of the arena...but ANDREW OLDHAM said "No, it's alright."

Latest kick with singers seems to be to take up photography...among those sporting cameras during the festival were DEWEY MARTIN, STEVE SILLS, MIKE WILLIAMS and DINK (of The KNACK).

SEEN AT THE FESTIVAL...DAVID CROSBY of the BYRDS and PAUL KANTER of the JEFFERSON AIRPLANE wandering through the booths...The MOBY GRAPE feeding chocolate chip cookies, which had far more than chocolate chips in them, to their manager... Former Action Kid MIKE WILLIAMS standing backstage as though looking for someone...JOHNNY RIVERS gone hippie in white pants, blue turtle neck sweater and soft white vesty thing lined and edged in grey fur.

SIMON AND GARFUNKLE singing ""I wish I were a corn flake'' and BRIAN JONES asleep in the audience. .PAUL BUTTERFIELD of P.B. Blues Band, and DAVID CROSBY on stage applauding the MIKE BLOOMFIELD THING, a relatively unknown blues band who rocked the festival...JIM MCQUINN introducing himself to the festival audience with ""Hi, I'm Roger'' and CHRIS HILLMAN wearing what was probably supposed to be an (India) Indian outfit but bore a strong resemblence to the old Dr Kildare shirts.

RUSS GUIGERE of the Association trying to make it to Big Sur but being stopped by too much traffic and fellow Associate BRIAN COLE saving your starving FLIP reporter by swiping sandwiches and cokes from artists' club.

In the audience to see and hear RAVI SHANKAR-- BRIAN JONES, DEWEY MARTIN, STEVE SILLS, several ANIMALS, most of the ASSOCIATION, JIM MCQUINN, CHRIS HILLMAN, DAVID CROSBY, PAUL SIMON, JOHNNY RIVERS, CASS, JOHN AND MICHELL, most of the JEFFERSON AIRPLANE and just about every other recording artist at the festival.

The festival opened with the ASSOCIATION and "Enter The Young'' and closed with the MAMAS AND PAPAS and "Dancing in the Streets,'' both of which are a fair indication of what went on during a most beautiful weekend in Monterey.

Next issue--complete details of the Pop Festival including the two guitars that were smashed on stage, the flowers and carrots that were given out and what made the whole festival worth while for Paul Simon.

MONKEES ARCHIVES 3

Flying with The Monkees is lots of fun! Experienced travelers all, Davy, Micky, Mike and Peter probably log more miles than many pilots! Here, at the beginning of a flight, Davy looks back at Mike, who pretends not to notice him by reading.

UP IN THE AIR WITH THE MONKEES!

Davy's changed seats now, so that he can turn around and have a go at Micky while Mr. D. is finishing his lunch.

In a different seat again, Davy breaks up at a scene in the aisle...

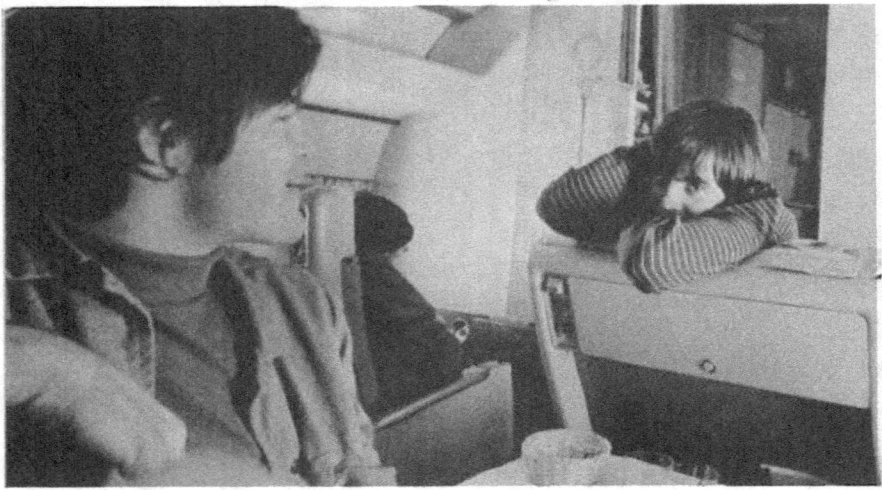

Peter looks weary as he rests on a pillow, his jacket covering him. The continuous strain of jet-speed traveling does get to the guys every so often, which is understandable. They all practically live on vitamin pills.

... Which finally totally convulses him in laughter!

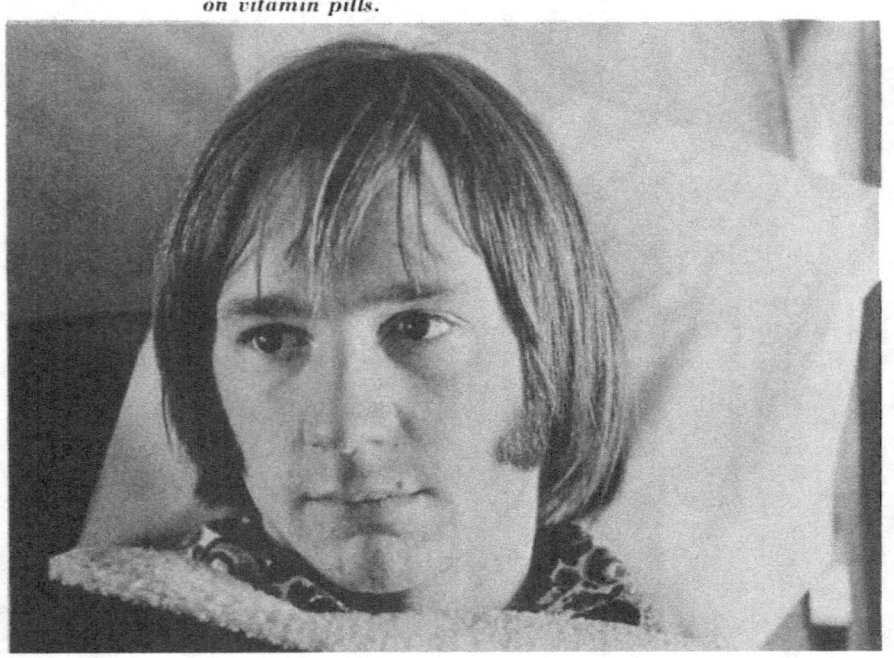

MONKEES ARCHIVES 3

Wearing an out-sized policeman's cap, Micky casually snaps on his seat belt and keeps on reading a comic book.

By the time the comic gets to Davy, it's kinda dogeared.

But the comic gets to Davy, giving him a worried moment or two.

Landed, with show time only hours off, the guys make it to their hotel safely. And, if they can, they flake out for a quick nap. Which is what Peter and Mike are doing right here.

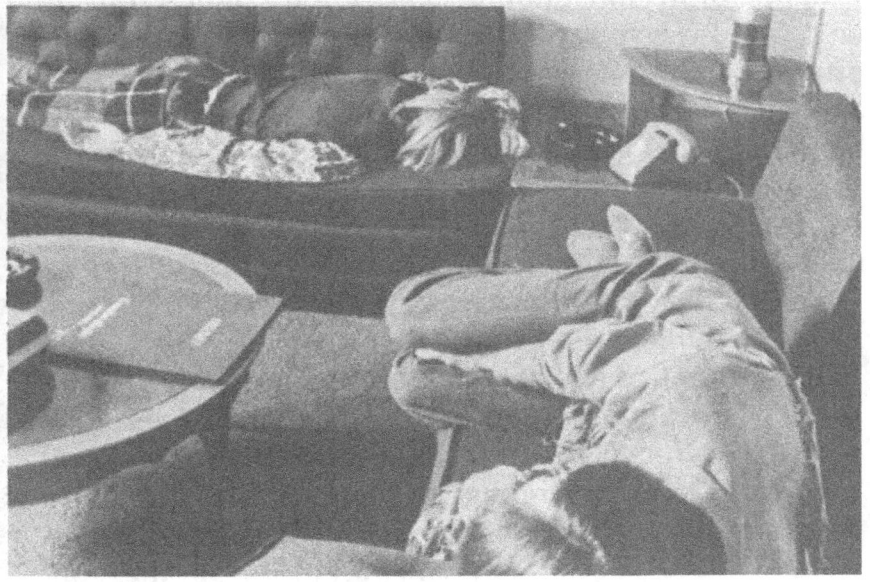

MONKEES ARCHIVES 3

MY COLLEGE DAYS WITH

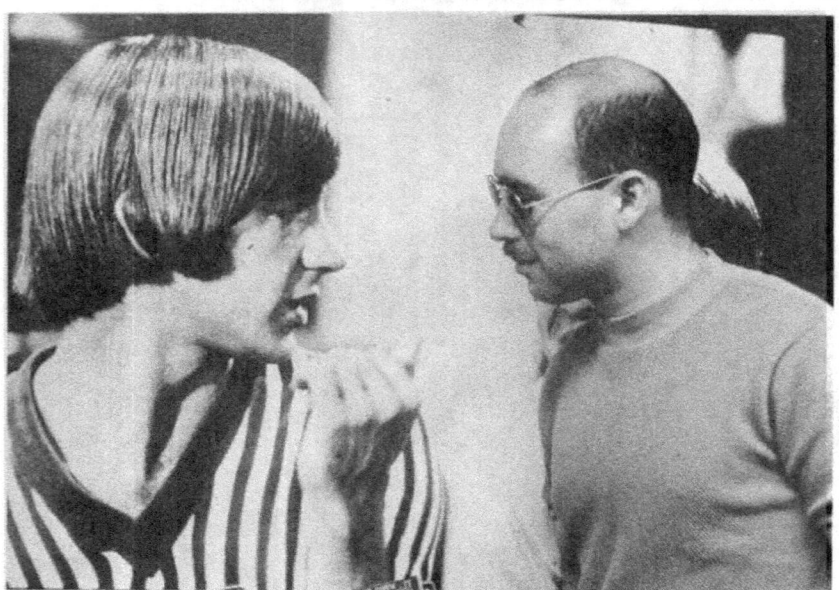

Peter's changed since his college days with Steve. And here Steve gets a brand-new, close-up view of his famous friend. "He looks basically the same as he did in college," says Steve, who was called "Poper" by Peter during the years they were best friends on campus.

In September, 1959, Peter H. Thorkelson entered Carleton College in Northfield, Minnesota. Steve Pope was a member of that same freshman class, and was graduated from Carleton in June, 1963. Peter, of course, never graduated, having already decided that music meant more to him than anything else in the world. But, during the two years that Peter did attend Carleton, his best friend on campus was "Poper"—Steve Pope, who shared all of Peter's happy and unhappy times. In an exclusive series beginning in this issue of FLIP, Steve will take you through these exciting years of Peter's life.

I'd just moved into Carleton's freshman dorm, when I saw Peter for the first time. Wearing short hair, looking very puckish and plucking on one of his oldest banjos, there he was — in one of his most familiar poses. I was to see Peter often like this. It seemed as if that banjo never left him!

We weren't introduced yet, but a couple of days later I found out that we were in the same math class together and that Peter's room was just down the hall from mine. Soon, I was introduced to Peter H. Thorkelson, beginning a friendship with Peter which lasted even long after he eventually left Carleton.

Funny about that name. You'd never think that there could be two Peter Thorkelsons in any one place at the same time. But there were actually two Peter Thorkelsons in my freshman class. The only difference was their middle initials and the fact that Peter pronounced the first part of his name "TORK" while the other pronounced his "Thork." Peter usually used his middle initial to keep their identities separate.

Right away, I knew that Peter was OK. Sophomores at Carleton haze the freshmen, but Peter would have no part of it from the start. Like, for instance, he re-

MONKEES ARCHIVES 3

PETER TORK! By STEVE POPE
Peter's Best Friend in College

fused to wear the beanie that all freshmen were supposed to wear to show the world their inferior status. Then, as always, Peter kept his cool!

I got to know Peter's room down the hall from mine very well. Banjos and guitars were hanging all over the walls. (But this room was nothing compared to the room Peter would have during his sophomore year! Which I'll talk about when I get to that period of Peter's life.)

The reason I got to know Peter's room so well is that he loved to stay up all night to talk about philosophy and politics, and those of us who shared Peter's thoughts usually did so in his room. There he would talk about anything that came to his crowded and creative mind. In old faded Levis, wearing a straight T-shirt (for some reason, during his freshman year, Peter always wore faded blue-and-white horizontally-striped T-shirts), with his banjo nearby, Peter would talk...and talk...and talk.

By the time Pete would be finished talking, you were convinced that what

MONKEES ARCHIVES 3

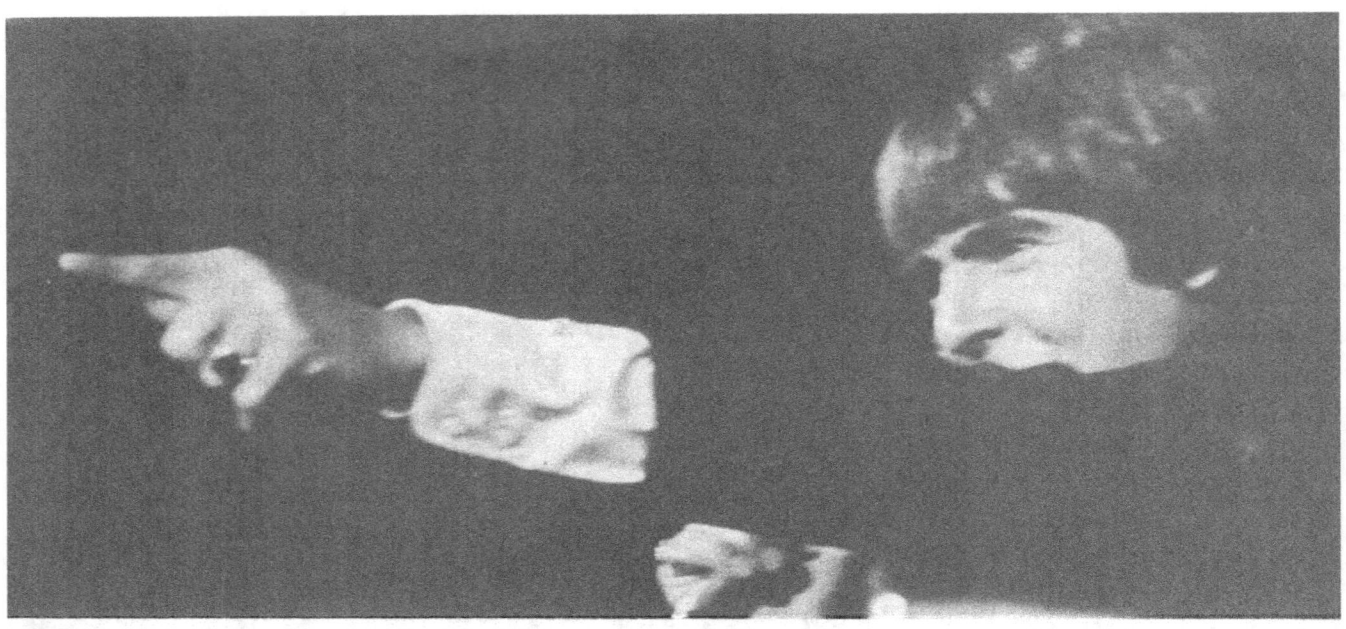

ON TOUR WITH THE MONKEES!

Have THE MONKEES come to your town yet?

This is what a visit by the fab four is like...

MONKEES ARCHIVES 3

Here, Davy and Micky check out the auditorium where they'll be performing that evening. Every stage has its own special problems, which The Monkees have to work out so that their spec sound doesn't change from city to city. If this groovy tour didn't convince everyone that each of The Monkees plays their own instruments, then nothing ever will!

ON TOUR WITH THE MONKEES!

Photos by Greg Gaston

The biggest problem for the guys is coming and going — without getting hurt. In each city, at every show, The Monkees have to scramble for safety. Here, Davy and Micky get ready to rush backstage. Peter, traveling in a second car, can be seen in the background.

Doing two things at once, Mike works on another mike while giving the crowd a quick once-over. Both the microphone and the crowd flipped for Mike!

Breathless and sweating, Peter pauses for a second on-stage, ready to give the crowd even more madness and music! If you've been lucky enough to see it, you know what kind of a great and groovy show they put on!

MONKEES ARCHIVES 3

Responding to the crowd, Micky grabs the microphone off the stand and flips out with another song!

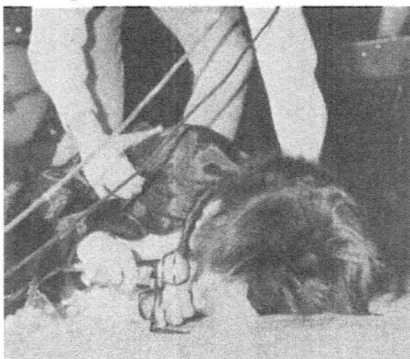

Micky gets carried away and gives it everything he's got!

This is what it would look like if you were on stage with The Monkees!

Micky getting ready for the action!

Tambourine in hand, Davy swings out . . .

In a different get-up, Davy keeps go-go-going! Which is really what Davy, Mike, Micky and Peter have been doing all summer!

TRAVEL WITH THE MONKEES! FLIP TO PAGE 62 FOR ANOTHER EXCLUSIVE OF THE MONKEES ON TOUR!

MONKEES ARCHIVES 3

Have We Misjudged THE MONKEES?

Hey, hey its the Monkees---and they've made a delightful film. I loved "Head," just loved every minute of it. And when the lights went on in the screening room and all the RCA and Colgems execs blinked their eyes at the applause I felt more than just a little tinge of remorse at the way the rock and roll press establishment has repeatedly blasted the Monkees.

Davy Jones ran to the front of the room anxiously asking some friends if they liked the film. Peter Tork, obscure behind a mangy new beard looked a little uncertain, too. I tend to think, and not without some chagrin-by-association, that the press is responsible for a lot of unpleasant changes Dolenz, Nesmith, Jones and Tork have been through as individuals.

Pop lacks perspective, as anything this newly successful must at first. A quick check of the critical criteria of the other arts, literature, theatre, TV and film shows these areas of creative expression far more understanding of the demands placed on its performing contingent. I say the Monkees have been misjudged, have been scored on the wrong

MONKEES ARCHIVES 3

Forgotten is the fact that they are actors playing rock and roll musicians, not the other way around. And if their music was at first prefabricated, well, that was where the TV show was at, and what of it. I really loved "Last Train to Clarksville", even before I knew the name of the group singing it. And when it was revealed that the Monkees weren't making any of the music ascribed to them I remember the outrage and hostility that followed in the press. At this juncture, (when it seems the whole pop movement has momentarily lost direction) that whole riff seemed kind of silly. Does anyone mind the instruments on Sgt. Pepper that the Beatles don't play?

Of course, the Monkees aren't the Beatles and they, like everyone else in the music scene with the possible exception of Frank Zappa (who is in Head) and Van Dyke Parks (who is not) will probably never even come close. But the Monkees aren't even barking up the same tree and to downrate them for that is pure rock and roll snobbery, a brand of hip-contempt that has become a revealing manifestation of the life style of the beautiful people.

As actors the Monkees have always excelled and they do endearingly well in "Head." They break in and out of character in a flicker of an instant, giving the little vignettes dramatic contrasts in perspective and unsettling breaks in mood. In the space of a few moments, each of the Monkees can switch from camp to black humor, to self conscious reality and back to histrionics, and make those changes smoothly, appropriately and professionally. What was attempted in "Magical Mystery Tour" is joyfully perfected in "Head."

The film opens with the titles and a song by the Monkees which in addition to being a catchy song is an unapologetic statement of where the film, and inevitably, the Monkees are at. "We're made out of tin," the song rejoices, "we're a manufactured product," it laments. Enjoy us for what we are, they demand, don't chastise us for what "Head," and, by extension The Monkees are not. The song goes on to explain that the film has no story, but a lot of stories, "its more fun that way." And they're right.

The director has looked at "Help," "A Hard Day's Night," and "Tom Jones" and learned from all of them. The photography is unexcelled, save perhaps by certain moments of "2001." And the high pitch of exhillaration the film embodies as it moves from one flash to the next, cross-connecting, self-parodying, cutting from realism to surrealism, never letting a laugh go by, makes it one of the most delightful experiences you could chose, a good cut above the majority of pop

MONKEES ARCHIVES 3

records that have been released in the past year.

One of the things that impressed me the most while watching the film, and indeed what inspired me to write this, my first film review, was the subtle apology by the Monkees for their career which hung subtly on the periphery of the sequences. The Monkees celebrated their own placticity while revealing for all to see their own contempt for 'media-truth,' and by the same token, their willing enslavement to it. The cameo roles of Victor Mature, Frank Zappa and Annette Funicello are used to imply a sort of backhanded defense of the kind of success the Monkees have attained. In one of the sequences, a Monkee Concert is intercut with war scenes, in another Frank Zappa (leading a bull around) confronts them and tells them the teen-agers of the world are depending on them. Think of the absurdity of Zappa's title for one of the Mothers' albums: "We're only in it for the Money." Think of the absurdity of anyone in the rock-scene pretending that money doesn't matter at all. Then dig the Monkees and the glass house they've had to live in because of some kind of dumb pop double standard.

Hey, hey this is not the best of all possible worlds. TV probably never will have the freedom of expression that albums now enjoy. If you've ever dreamed of, or tried to pursue a creative profession you know all too well the contradictions and conflicts that face you once you've earned an audience of your own. Unless of course you are as bit as the Beatles and already *there*, a rebel with more power behind you than above you.

John Lennon stands naked and humble, nude and proud on the face of an album cover while Country Joe and the Fish and the Fugs thought of it a year or two ago but their respective record companies wouldn't hear of it. Regardless of how you feel about nudity, the analogy makes it point. There are the Monkees, naked in their images, telling it like their bosses said it should be. And in Head, by overstatement and inversion, telling it like it is. The point is, Head, in its own way is an honest and occasionally incisive movie, technically brilliant and aesthetically beautiful. More importantly, it's a lot of fun. And it's worthy of a good sight more respect than it's probably going to get. And that's a shame.

Hey, hey go see "Head." And enjoy yourselves? The Monkees would like it that way---and they've made no bones about it. □ellen sander

MONKEES ARCHIVES 3

How The

Because the Monkees' homes are the only places where they are *not* Monkees, Davy Jones, Peter Tork, Micky Dolenz and Mike Nesmith have probably put more of their real selves into their homes than any other facet of their lives. For this reason, by taking a look at how they live you can actually see a little more of the person behind the image.

More than any of the other Monkees, Mike's home is a total extension of his philosophy and the realization of the dreams he had of "home" as a boy.

POOR CHILDHOOD

Mike grew up in the very poor section of Dallas, Texas. His mother worked to raise her son like other children, but still Mike felt the sting of having raggedy clothes, the feeling of hunger and the hope of something better for him and his mother.

Along with Mike's longing for something better came his present philosophy which is greatly influenced by his religion, Christian Science. Both he and his wife, Phyllis, believe that if you desire material things and you have them, then they become less important. So, they spared no expense in building their beautiful home.

MIKE'S GORGEOUS HOME is what he's always wanted. The peace and quiet that Phyllis needs to raise the children is right here. There's a lovely yard to run in and the privacy Mike needs to do his composing. The Nesmiths have also become very gracious entertainers at home. It's a groovy experience to be invited here for a party.

Monkees Live

PETER'S PAD
Peter Tork lives in the smallest and simplest house of all the four Monkees. He has mentioned, "When I went to look for my first house I thought of hills and cool green." And so he found it.

Material objects to Peter are the least important things in his life, so his house and its furnishings are simple, yet very, very comfortable. Peter is currently looking for a bigger place since his current house can't accommodate all his friends.

MONKEES ARCHIVES 3

MICKY'S WONDERLAND

Micky Dolenz has a "thing" about children—he loves them, he loves their fairy tales and he would love to be one again. The house in which he lives is probably the closest he'll come to returning to childhood himself.

Mick's house sits half-way up a steep hill in Laurel Canyon and looks like a cross between a Swiss Chalet and the gingerbread house from Hanzel and Gretel. He's currently building treehouses for the trees behind his house; and when he entertains he's a very warm host who makes sure that everyone is having fun at all times. He serves his guests popsicles of all flavors and entertains them by showing movies like "Alice in Wonderland" in color. But as you can see, Micky's house is a wonderland all on its own.

MONKEES ARCHIVES 3

ENGLISH COTTAGE

If Davy Jones' house is an extension of him, as he says it is, then you'll know right away his heart is still in England. He chose the house he now owns because to him it looked like an English country house.

At first Davy had a full-time housekeeper and cook, but when he missed doing those things himsef, he let them go. Now he does almost everything himself. This is one of the ways Davy relaxes. Like the other Monkees, the times they seem to enjoy most are those spent at home with friends and family, because the houses themselves are sort of friends, too!

www.ingramcontent.com/pod-product-compliance
Lightning Source LLC
Chambersburg PA
CBHW080814190426
43197CB00041B/2804